# The Spiritual Stamina For End-Time Christians

# The Spiritual Stamina For End-Time Christians

IT TAKES STAMINA
TO FINISH THE RACE

**Freeson U. Eze**

F.U.E Publication

# Contents

# Copyright

# DEDICATION

This book is dedicated to all believers in Christ Jesus over the entire world and to God's servants in the fivefold ministry in the church of Jesus Christ.

# ACKNOWLEDGEMENT

I sincerely thank the omnipotent God for bestowing on me the knowledge and divine talent necessary to write this book.

In addition, I want to thank my wife, Queen Eze, for all of her help and inspiration while I was writing this book. I value the contributions you make.

I appreciate the editing staff's work on the manuscript. My appreciation also extends to Apostle and Mrs. Chuks Eze for all the help you all provided me with during the writing of this book.

I want to express my gratitude to Rev. J. Akpovino and all members of the Gospel Believers Mission branch in Ajangbadi. I want to express my gratitude to every person in the Christ General Prayer and Evangelical Movement.

I want to express my sincere gratitude to Gen. and Mrs. Ezra J. Jakko, the general overseers of Gospel Believers Mission, as well as to all the ministers and pastors of this great commission, GBM.

# *Preface.*

In January 2019, about a few days after the New Year's celebration, I had a revelation (a dream) that stunned me for weeks. I awoke from the dream and couldn't get myself together for days. This is what I saw.

"In the dream, as I was returning from seeing some of my church members, something in the sky caught my attention. When I look at it, I see that those were cars, big trucks, and tanks, so I thought to myself that science had advanced because they had created flying cars.

So, as I watched intently, I noticed people in the sky being carried by strong winds; this is when I realized those cars were also being carried by the wind.

Then, as I turned to look up, I noticed the wind blowing in my direction. I immediately began to run, but I was unable to move as quickly as I had anticipated. Then the wind picked me up and carried me away, but my hands were still holding onto the pillar and my legs were inverted. I held onto the pillar that I was holding while yelling, "Lord Jesus, have mercy on me," and the wind was so strong that I could see it sweeping various vehicles, including cars, trucks, and heavy machinery. I didn't let go of the pillar that I was holding. I kept clinging to the pillar. I finally awakened.

As I woke up, what I was hearing in my heart was "THE END-TIME WIND IS BLOWING, AND MY CHILDREN NEED STAMINA TO WITHSTAND," and another voice spoke to my heart. ("Note this down; end-of-day stamina is required.") Then I wrote down the whole dream, thinking that was all until 2020, when COVID-19 hit the entire world.

In 2020, however, the Lord's spirit prompted me once more, saying, "I asked you to write that book down, but you're kidding." My heart truly opened up when I realised that the Holy Spirit wants me to write a book that even the next generation of believers will read about. But I wrote it, so I took out my notebook and reread the dream.

The second dream I had happened about 15 years ago, when I was very young in my faith, and I never understood it, but after my dream in 2019, I understood it more clearly. The spirit of the Lord brought back the memory of this dream and gave me understanding.

In the dream, I was kneeling for prayer but fell asleep, and as the Lord Jesus walked in, I raised my head and I just knew it was Jesus; there aren't enough words to describe how gracious He is and the brightness of the light that is in Him.

As I look at him, he smiles at me, and then lots of questions run through my mind, but I only ask Jesus one question, which is, "Lord Jesus, will I enter your kingdom?" He was smiling at me and said, "I don't know. Work hard." I was like, "Why will Jesus not know?" He gave me the same answer after I asked him the same question again. I asked him again a third time, and this time I was crying. He looked at me with a smile and said the same thing.

Then Jesus walked away from me, but I was still looking at him as he was going. Jesus was checking on some other believers in the neighbourhood, and they didn't know He was looking at them, so I started calling at them. I was screaming at them, saying, "The Lord Jesus is watching you guys," but only a few were paying attention. I kept yelling until I woke up.

In order to shout to the world and to all believers that Jesus is watching, I wrote this book. Additionally, I was receiving additional teachings from the Holy Spirit that I had never known or understood before.

I wrote this book to address the carefree lifestyle of Christians in these last days and to remind the church again that the church is the body of Jesus and not of herself.

to awaken the sleeping virgin in the church, to warn against and correct certain things that last-day believers do that are making them so weak. That was the reason for writing this book?

The question of why so many people's prayers go unanswered is also covered in this book. And why, despite the fact that there are so many churches, especially in Africa, are sin and sinners growing even within the churches?

Why have pastors become bland? The true leadership test was lost by them. Some ministers are starting to take Jesus' words seriously.

("The blind leading the blind"), and we know both will end in destruction.

**The Challenge.**

When I started writing this book, I was not consistent due to having too many activities to keep up with. So I started writing with my phone through an app called Notepad. And everything was fine because I was now writing daily as the spirit prompted me. So after about six chapters, the Holy Spirit prompted me again to copy everything to my system or hard drive, but I ignored it, and as I continued writing the next chapter, my phone got damaged and I couldn't access anything in it.

That was how I lost everything, and I was so discouraged with myself for days. After some days, I started praying and asking God for help, and He truly helped me. I could recall some, but not the majority. Unless you are an author and a writer, you may not understand the agony of losing about six chapters of your writing.

This book is a must-read for every Christian who truly longs for the truth and seeks to finish his or her race well.

# Introduction.

*The great dragon—the ancient serpent, the one called Devil and Satan, the one who led the whole earth astray—was thrown out, and all his angels were thrown out with him, thrown down to earth. Revelation 12:7–12 MSG*

I welcome criticism. Because Satan was referred to as a serpent in Genesis 3, he has been engaged in the practice of deceit for thousands of years and has progressed from Genesis to Exodus to Leviticus to Deuteronomy, according to a very careful study of this very Bible verse. As a result, what we have in this final age is like "an updated and upgraded devil," so to speak. He is referred to as "that great dragon" in Revelation, changing the word "serpent" to "dragon."

The Bible took great care to refer to him as "the great dragon." But the disciples stood firm against the dragon; the gospel was preached in the presence of the old serpent, and they succeeded because they learned how to build spiritual stamina in their time from their master.

Although it won't be through strength or might, I can only imagine the stamina it will take to resist a dragon. However, I can assure you that the disciples of old had the inner strength necessary to resist and maintain control over themselves in the face of the dragon's might.

Don't tell me that Satan, the great dragon, hasn't improved or updated both his cunning and deceit since the time of the book of Revelation, which was written over two thousand years ago.

The Bible says, "For we wrestle not against flesh and blood."

If there is wrestling, then there is a need to build spiritual stamina.

*Endings are better than beginnings. Sticking to it is better than standing out. Ecclesiastes 7:8 MSG*

The beginning of anything and everything is important, but the end of anything and everything is most important. That's why the Bible said

*Finishing is better than starting. Patience is better than pride. Ecclesiastes 7:8 NLT*

It's great to have a solid foundation for a house to be built on, but if the house cannot be finished to the desired standard, the foundation is useless and a waste of resources. Meaning? Simply being born again does not ensure that you will enter heaven.

For years, I have pondered the nature of life, wondering why, when a child is born, only that child sobs while everyone else around him or her laughs and rejoices, but when that same child, who has since grown into an adult, passes away years later, only he or she remains silent in the coffin while everyone else sobs in sympathy. Understand why?

Listen, one of the reasons every child normally cries at birth is that it marks the beginning of his or her life.

1. He or she is unsure of whether they will make God happy at the end of their lives. Therefore, the Bible states:

*"I knew you before I formed you in your mother's womb. "Before you were born, I set you apart and appointed you as my prophet to the nations." Jeremiah 1:5 NLT*

1. He or she is unsure of whether they will be welcomed home by their creator after spending time on earth.

*Life, while lovely while it lasts, is soon over. Life, as we know it, is precious and beautiful. They put the body back in the same ground it came from. The spirit returns to God, who first breathed it. Ecclesiastes 12:6–7 MSG*

1. The child crying at birth is wondering if he will be able to complete the task assigned to him by God.

The Bible says this about the life of the apostle Paul.

*You take over. I'm about to die, my life an offering on God's altar. This is the only race worth running. I've run hard right to the finish and believed all the way. All that's left now is the shouting—God's applause! Depend on it; he's an honest judge. He'll do right not only by me but by everyone eager for his coming. 2 Timothy 4:6–8 MSG.*

1. The child's sobs are another indication that he has experienced the struggle of life and what lies ahead.

*Man that is born of a woman is of few days, and full of trouble. Job 14:1 KJV*

*"How frail is humanity! How short is life, how full of trouble! Job 14:1 NLT.*

Every baby born or that will be born normally may experience all of these things, and if a child is born without crying, the doctor and nurse will make sure they do something to cause the child to cry.

So it is with our faith in God: it is one thing to repent and receive the free gift of salvation, but it is quite another to maintain it until the end.

This book appears to bring to the reader the reality and importance of finishing well and to reveal certain hidden truths that will inspire him to rise and fight to finish, but not just finish, but to finish well. like the Bible said.

*The end of something is better than its beginning. Patience is better than pride. Ecclesiastes 7:8 GNT*

This book explains how one can finish well and also demonstrates that one needs stamina to finish anything well because it will not be simple. And in this book, you will learn why the first Christians succeeded in finishing their race and why Christians today are faltering and failing to succeed, allowing you to avoid the errors they made.

**The Reason for This Book**

"When the blind lead the blind," we all know how that ends.

After some revelations, I finally understood some questions that I had been asking myself for a long time. This book attempts to address some of these issues.

The questions are:

1. Why are there so many churches now, but with little or no results to show?
2. Why do Christians, especially men of God of my generation, including me, seem to lack the power and authority the disciples of old had?
3. Wasn't it the same Jesus Christ who was preached about by the apostles Peter, Paul, John, and others, and who we are preaching about today?
4. Has God ceased to be God?

5: Has the word of God changed and lost value in this end-time?

1. What exactly did the older generation of Christians do that gave them such power and enabled them to transform entire countries?
2. Where and how have we fallen short in this generation, causing modern sceptics to deride the gospel and our Christian faith?

8: Why do there seem to be so many churches and so many sinners? I mean, churches everywhere, and sinners growing in number?

1. Why does it appear that the church has devolved into an entertainment venue, with some pastors even inviting comedians to their altars?

10: Why has Christianity in my generation become so trivial in the eyes of non-believers?

11: Who has bewitched us? Etc.

I have a lot of questions in my head that need answers, including those listed above. A voice in my heart said, "Stamina for the end of time is required" at this point. Have you got the endurance? I speak of spiritual stamina as a believer. And the endurance to see this world through?

**The Author's Request**

I dedicate this book to the church of Jesus Christ and the believers of these last days, so if it has been a blessing to you, kindly use it or give it as a gift to others.

# 1

# *Time vs. stamina*

The Power of Time

Nobody was born as an adult. We were all born as babies before we grew to become adults. Nobody also becomes a champion or giant as soon as he is born. Neither do seeds become trees overnight. Everything in life goes through a maturing or achieving greatness process. We know the period through which individuals grow to become something and the space of that growth as "time." In this chapter, I want to talk about the importance of the process of life.

Someone once said, "Time heals all wounds," and I agree in one sense because time can also cause damage and create wounds that are difficult to heal. What I mean is that an ugly girl can mature into a beautiful woman over time, and a beautiful woman can also age. What I mean is that an ugly girl can mature into a beautiful woman over time, and a beautiful woman can also age. The key thing here is that time changes the form and shape of individuals. It increases and reduces the glory of men and kingdoms. Those who were beautiful and strong some years ago, when they were 20–30 years old, cannot look the same at seventy. Their youthful figure and strength have dwindled.

Everything God created is subject to Him because He existed outside of the dimensions of time and space. The law of time does not limit God. It is the reason the Bible says:

*"Jesus Christ is eternally [changeless] the same yesterday, today, and forever." Hebrew 13:8 AMP.*

*"Jesus Christ, the same as yesterday, today, and forever." Hebrew 13:8 KJV*

The above scripture states clearly that God is eternal and does not change. He can change time and seasons, directing the affairs of the universe. He can accomplish this because he exists outside of time and space.

Whether or not people believe in his existence, God continues to control the world—in fact, the entire universe—through time and the seasons he created. For someone to be successful in any field of endeavour, he needs stamina that can sustain him. We gain stamina through training and development. The same thing applies to our Christian faith. In the sower's parable, Jesus said some people received the word of God with joy, but they have no root; they only endure for a while. When afflictions and challenges come to test them, they become offended and abandon their faith. [Matthew 13:20-21]. They faded away because they had no stamina to continue the race. I want us to see three different Bible translations for a better understanding of this issue.

1. *"Listen to the [meaning of the] parable of the sower:*
2. *When anyone hears the word of the kingdom (regularly salvation) and does not understand and grasp it, the evil one comes and snatches away what was sown in his heart. This is the person whose seed was planted alongside the road.*
3. *On whom a seed was sown on rocky ground This is the one who hears the word and at once welcomes it with joy.*

*21 But he has no stamina rooted in himself; it is only temporary, and when pressure or persecution comes from the word, he stumbles and falls away [abandoning the source of salvation].*

*22 And the one on whom seed was sown among the thorns, this is the one who hears the word, but the cares and distractions of the word and deceitfulness [the superficial pleasure and delight] of riches choke the word and it yield no fruit.*

*23 And the one on whom seed was sown on the good soil, this is the one who hears the word and understands and grasp it: he indeed bears fruit and yield some hundred time [as much as was sown], some sixty [times as much], and some thirty." Matthew 13:18-23 AMP*

*18 "Now listen to the explanation of the parable about the farmer planting seeds.*

*19 The seed that fell on the footpath represents those who hear the message of the kingdom but don't understand it. Then the evil one comes and snatches away the seed that was planted in their hearts.*

*20 The seed on the rocky soil represents those who hear the message and immediately receive it with joy.*

*But since they don't have deep roots, they didn't last long. They fall away as soon as they have problems or are persecuted for believing it. The seed that fell among the thorns represents those who hear God's word.*

*22 But all too quickly the message is crowded out by the worries of this life and the lure of wealth, so no fruit is produced.*

*23 "The seed that fell on good soil" represents those who truly hear and understand God's word and produce a harvest of thirty, sixty, or even a hundred times as much as had been planted. Matthew 13:18-23NLT*

*"Study this story of the farmer planting seed. When anyone hears news of the kingdom and doesn't take it in, it just remains on the surface, and so the evil one comes along and plucks it right out of that person's heart. This is the seed the farmer scatters on the road. The seed is cast in the gravel, and this is the person who hears it and instantly responds with enthusiasm. But there is no soil of character, and so when the emotions wear off and some difficulty arrives, there is nothing to show for it.""The seed cast in the weeds is the person who hears kingdom news, but weeds of worry and illusions about getting more and wanting everything under the sun strangle what was heard,*

*and nothing comes of it. ""The person who hears and absorbs the news and then produces a harvest beyond his wildest dreams is the seed cast on good soil." Matthew 13:18-23MSG*

Time is the key factor in building and developing anything that endures and is of great value. Using the criteria mentioned in the sower's parable, I want to divide believers into four groups.

They are:

- The roadside believers
- Rocky Ground believers
- Thorns ground believers
- Good ground, believers.

These are the four categories of Christians we have in the body of Christ [the church] today. As a Christian, when you critically look at the four categories I mentioned above, you will realise you belong to one of them.

1. The roadside believers

   The roadside believers are the church's first group of believers. These are the believers who serve God from a distance. This type of believer loves Christian gatherings, but they are not committed to the things of God, and the love of God is not in their hearts. They make up about 60% of the church membership. In my observation, this set of people is the type God told his prophet in the Bible; they came as my people come.

   *The master said, "These people make a big show of saying the right thing, but their hearts aren't in it. Because they act like they are worshiping me but don't mean it, I'm going to step in and shock them awake, astonish them, and turn them on their ears. The wise ones who had it all figured out will be exposed as fools. ""The smart people who thought they knew everything will turn out to know nothing." Isaiah 29:13-14MSG*

*The Lord said, "These people claim to worship me, but their words are meaningless, and their hearts are somewhere else. Their religion is nothing but human rules and traditions, which they have simply memorized. So I will sterilize them with one unexpected blow after another. ""Those who are wise will turn out to be fools, and all their cleverness will be useless." Isaiah 29:13-14GNT*

*"And they come unto thee as the people come, and they sit before thee as my people, and they hear the words, but they will not do them; for with their mouths they show much love, but their hearts go after their covetousness." Ezekiel 33:31 KJV*

*"Ye hypocrites, will did Esaias prophesy of you, saying, this people draweth nigh unto me with their mouth, and honoureth me with me with their lips but their hearts is far from me". Matthew 15:7-8 KJA*

The above Bible passages are to show that roadside believers are in the body of Christ, or church. The fact that they are in the church is no longer in dispute, but the worrisome aspect is that some of them have stayed too long in the church and are familiar with its systems and language. As a result, they spoke and acted like sheep when they were goats. Some of them are even in leadership positions in the church. It takes a spirit of discernment to find them out. If you have read through the different versions I used for my explanation, you will have discovered what God said about them. God is not happy with roadside believers; they render lip service to God and are only interested in religious rituals. Commitments and true worship are far from them.

2. Rocky Ground Believers

3. *"The seed on the rocky soil represents those who hear the message and immediately receive it with joy"*

4. *They don't last long, however, because they don't have deep roots. They fell away as soon as they had problems or were persecuted for believing God's word. "The seed that fell among the thorns represents those who hear God's word." Matthew 13:20-21*

The second group or class of Christians are the "rocky ground" Christians. In my estimation, they are the second largest in the church in terms of numbers. They are the group of believers who received the word of God with joy. This means that they love the word of God and want to serve God. But serving God entails more than just the thrill of the phrase.

One must have the stamina to do so, because they have no stamina. They crumble as soon as there is some shaking to demonstrate their belief in the word. They are quick to fall into temptation and backslide in their hearts while they are still in the church. They are also the compromise that makes Christian values cheap. You should know that they speak in tongues, preach the gospel, and render other services in the church. I think they make up about 20% of the church membership. Most believers in this group live in pretence and practice high levels of hypocrisy. It is important to note that most of the believers in this group did not become what they are intentionally. It was an attempt to avoid the trial of their faith in the word of God that made them stray into hypocrisy. The major reason for this is that they lacked the required stamina to withstand trial and temptation.

3. THE THORNS GROUND BELIEVERS

*"He also who received seed among thorns is he who heareth the word; but the cares of this world and the deceitfulness of riches choke the word, and he becomes unfruitful." Matthew 13:22KJV*

The thorny believers are the third group of believers. I want to define the word "thorn" and see how it applies to this parable. This will help us understand this context better. A thorn is a stiff, sharp-pointed woody projection on the stem or other part of a plant. or a sharp, rigid process on a plant, especially one that is short, indurated, sharp-pointed, and leafless.

The above definition of the thorn reveals that the church has a big problem to solve as regards its structure and membership. What Jesus Christ meant by "thorn" in the parable differs from the definition I have given. In reality, what we commonly regard as a beautiful life, riches, a wealthy lifestyle, and comfort are what Jesus Christ referred to as thorns.

The way we see and give meaning to things differs from God. Things we consider dangerous and frightening may be viewed as blessings by God. The desire to become wealthy and famous, as well as the desire for worldly glory, are perilous and frightening to a heavenly vision. But the ability to endure trial and temptation, which we do not appreciate, is what is pleasing to God, and it leads us to heaven. I put the membership of this group of believers at 15%. I don't want you to lose sight of what I'm doing here. The main reason I divide believers in Christ into different categories is to help you identify your own category and amend your ways. Hear what the Lord Jesus said to that group of believers.

*"And unto the angel of the church of the Laodiceans write: These things say the Amen, the faithful and true witness, the beginning of the creation of God; I know thy works that thou art neither cold nor hot; would thou be cold or hot? So then because thou are lukewarm and neither cold or hot, I will spew thee out of my mouth, because thou sayest, I am rich, and increased with goods, and have need of nothing; and knowest not that thou art wretched and miserable, and poor, and blind, and naked: I counsel thee to buy of me gold tried in the fire, that thou mayest be rich; and white raiment, that thou mayest be clothed and that the shame of thy nakedness do not appear; and anoint thy eyes with eyesalve, that thou mayest see. As many as I love, I rebuke and chasten; be zealous, therefore, and repent. Behold, I stand at the door and knock; if any man hears my voice and opens the door, I will come in to him and will sup with him, and he with me. To him that overcometh will I grant to sit with me in my throne, even as I also overcome, and am sit down with my father in his throne". Revelation 3:14-21KJV*

4. Good ground believers

The fourth and last group of believers found in the church are the "good ground" believers. This group or category of believers makes up the smallest percentage of the people who claim to worship God. I estimate their percentage to be 5 percent. The smallness of this group of believers accounted for the reason Jesus said:

*"Many are called, but few are chosen." Matthew 22:14 KJV*

This is the only group of Christians about which Jesus said He bore fruit.

*"The seed that fell on good soil" represents those who truly hear and understand God's word and produce a harvest of thirty, sixty, or even a hundred times as much as had been planted. Matthew13:23NLT*

From the above scripture, we can see that this category of believers actually produced fruit. The question one may ask is, "Why were they able to produce fruits? To answer this question correctly, you should know that the production of any valuable thing involves some processes. Processes take time, like hours, days, months, and years, which translates into time used. The message here is that this group of believers had stamina, and because of the stamina, they could overcome trials and temptations that came their way.

The consequences of their endurance and faith in the Word were that they produced fruits at different levels. some thirtyfold, according to God's grace in their lives. others sixty times, and the rest a hundred times. The hundredfold fruit-bearers probably tapped into the unlimited grace of Jesus Christ—that grace to do all things. It is not too late for you to bear fruit in the church if you are not bearing any currently. All you need to do is repent of your dead work.

And as a prodigal son, tell Jesus to give you a second chance to serve him better, and he will do so. As a good Christian, you need to know and understand certain truths that will help you worship God better.

**The Three Levels of a Worshipper**

A true worshipper of God can express his or her love for God in a variety of ways, depending on his or her circumstances, experience, and emotions. Here, I identify three levels at which people worship God. These are:

- Reasoning/Rational
- Revelational

• Emotional

Text: Matthew 16:13–26. From two verses of the Bible:

*"When Jesus arrived in the villages of Caesarea Philippi, he asked his disciple, "What are people saying about the son of man?" They replied, "Some think he is John the baptizer, some say Elijah, some say Jeremiah, or one of the other prophets. He pressed them, "And how about you?" "Who do you think I am?" Matthew 16:13-15MSG*

*"Simon Peter said, "You are the Christ, the messiah, the son of the living God." Matthew 16:16MSG*

*"Jesus came back, saying, "God bless you, Simon, son of Jonah! You didn't get the answer from the books or from the teacher. My father in heaven, God himself, let you in on this secret of who I really am. And now I'm going to tell everyone who you really are. You are Peter, a rock. This is the rock on which I will put together my church, a church so expensive with energy that not even the gates of hell will be able to keep it out". Matthew 16:17–18 MSG*

*"And that's not all. You will have completer and freer access to God's kingdom, keys to open any and every door—no more barriers between heaven and earth. "Yes" on earth is "yes" in heaven. "A no on earth is a no in heaven." Matthew 16:19MSG.*

*"Then Jesus made it clear to his disciples that it was now necessary for him to go to Jerusalem, submit to an ordeal of suffering at the hands of the religious leaders, be killed, and then on the last third day be raised up alive. Peter took him in hand, protesting, "Impossible, master! That can never be!" Matthew 16:21-22MSG.*

*"But Jesus wasn't severe." Peter, get out of my way. Satan, get lost. You have no idea how God works; get out of my way. Satan, get lost. You have no idea how God works. Matthew 16:23MSG*

*Then Jesus went to work on his disciples. " Anyone who intends to come with me has to let me level; you are not in the driver's seat; I am. Don't run from suffering; embrace it. Follow me, and I will show you how self-help is no* help at all. Self- service is the way, my way, to finding yourself, your true self. What kind of deal is it to get everything you want and lose yourself? What could you ever trade your soul for? Matthew 16:24-26MSG.

13 When Jesus came into the coast of Caesarea Philippi, he asked his disciple, saying "whom do men say that the son of man am?"

14 And they said, some say that thou are John the Baptist; some Elias, and other Jeremiah, or one of the prophets.

15 He said unto them, "But whom say ye that I am?"

16 And Simon Peter answered and said, "You are the Christ, the son of the living God."

17 And Jesus answered and said, unto him, Blessed art thou, Simon-Bar-Jona; for the flesh and the blood hath not revealed it to unto thee, but my father which is in heaven.

18 And I say also unto thee, thou art Peter, and upon this rock I will build my church, and the gates of hell shall not prevail against it.

19 And I will give unto thee the keys of the kingdom of heaven: And whatsoever thou shall bind on earth shall be bound in heaven: and whatsoever thou shall lose on earth shall be lose in heaven.

20 Then he charged his disciples that they should tell no one that he was Jesus the Christ.

21 From that time forth, Jesus began to show his disciples how he must go to Jerusalem and suffer many things from the elders, the chief priest, and the scribes, be killed, and be raised again the third day.

22 Then Peter took him and began to rebuke him, saying, "Be it far from thee Lord; this shall not be unto thee.

23 But he turned, and said unto Peter Get thee behind me, Satan; thou art an offence unto me for thou savourest not the things that be of God, but those of men."

24 Then said Jesus unto his disciples, "If any man will come after me, let him deny himself, take up his cross, and follow me."

*25 "For whosoever will save his life shall lose it, and whosoever will lose his life for my sake shall find it."*

*26 For what is man profited, if he shall gain the whole world and lose his own soul? Or what shall a man give in exchange for his soul? Matthew 16:13–26KJV.*

## 1. THE REASONING / RATIONAL WORSHIPPERS

Many people worship God according to what they think or feel. Their service to God is determined by what they think. They always try to be rational in all they do in the church. In the scriptures we read above, Jesus asked his disciples what people thought of him. The disciples replied that the opinion of the people about the personality of Christ was based on their thinking. According to the disciples, some thought he was Elijah, John the Baptist, or the prophet.

Being able to reason is a very useful activity and exercise, but when it is applied to worshipping God, we may not achieve our purpose and plan with God. Reasoning or rational worshippers cannot hear from God and may struggle to please Him. This is because they must have some justification based on certain calculations before they do anything serious in the church. The Holy Spirit cannot lead such worshippers because God does not listen to human reasons to decide. These are the Christian apostle Paul called babies.

*"But for right now, friends, I'm completely frustrated by your unspiritual dealings with each other and with God. You are acting like infants in relation to Christ, capable of nothing much more than nursing at the breast. "Well then, I'll nurse you since you don't seem capable of anything more.""As long as you go for what makes you feel good or makes you look important, are you really much different than a babe at the breast, content only when everything is going your way?" 1 Corinthians3:1-3KJV*

From the above scriptures, we learn that Apostle Paul described some believers of his day as "babies in Christ" because of their reasoning ability. The apostle Paul had taught them the word of God, and they believed. When they saw the apostles, who were also teachers of the word, some claimed to belong to the apostles, while others claimed to belong to Paul. Paul was not happy with their reasoning capacity. He rebuked them and let them know that the word of God is spiritual. It is not something one can apply his reasoning faculty to achieve as a divine result. Some years ago, someone told me to serve God with the number six. I asked him what the number six was, and he told me it was the brain. The question I asked him then was: If God, who created us, gave us the number six, what number is God using as the creator of humankind? My question created confusion in his mind because he could not answer it.

He returned to me a few months later and told me that no one can serve God faithfully with their brain, or number six. God gave us a brain to think with so that we could live well. We cannot apply the method of our daily reasoning to our service to God. It is dangerous because the devil can hijack our reasoning system and use it against us and God. In the book Job, we see how the wife of Job was reasoning out the situation around her husband. As she was processing her thoughts, the devil gave her an idea he had told God before. I want you to recall that the devil boasted that Job would curse God if God allowed him to suffer beyond a certain limit. His wife said,

*"You're still holding on to your precious integrity, are you? ""Curse God and be done with it." He told her, "You are talking like an empty-headed fool. ""We take the good days from God; why not the bad days as well?" Not once through all this did Job sin. He said nothing against God. Job 2:9-10MSG*

The devil always hijacks the reasoning faculties of men; even though what they want to do is good, through craftiness, the devil will turn it into evil. We should not forget that the devil is the prince of the air. What does that mean? It means that the devil controls the airwaves through which reasoning travels.

It was not surprising when the devil whispered his plan to the ear of Job's wife. The plan of the devil was for Job to curse God, and when the woman said, "Curse God," the devil spoke through her. The devil could use her because she attempted to reason out the calamity that befell her husband, even though he was a righteous man. It is not only her; any believer who dwells in the realm of reason in his walk with Christ is likely to become a victim of devil manipulation.

This was the trap that caught Eve at the beginning of time; instead of obeying the word of God, Eve engaged herself in reasoning and unnecessary dialogue with the devil. What was the outcome? She became the victim of her lust and foolish reasoning, selling the whole human race into suffering, slavery, and death.

*The serpent was clever—more clever than any wild animal God had made. He spoke to the woman, saying, "Do I understand that God told you not to eat from any tree in the Garden? Genesis 3:1MSG.*

*The woman said to the serpent, "Not at all. We can eat from the trees in the garden. It's only about the tree in the middle of the garden that God said, "Don't eat from it; don't even touch it, or you will die." Genesis 3:2-3MSG.*

*The serpent told the woman, "You won't die; God knows that the moment you eat from that tree, you will see what's really going on. ""You will be just like God, knowing everything, ranging all the way from good to evil." Genesis 3:4-5MSG.*

*"When the woman saw that the tree looked like good food and realized what she would get out of it, she would know everything!" "She took and ate the plant, and then she gave some to her husband, and he ate," Genesis 3:6 MSG.*

The scriptures we have read above show that Eve took time to reason and saw some advantages in her decision to eat the fruit before she did so. Those who want to worship God through reasoning will always see the advantages they will gain from doing so. Such a group of worshippers will not see the disadvantages of not obeying the word of God.

## 2. REVELATIONAL WORSHIPPERS

*15 He said unto them, "But whom say ye that I am?"*

*16 And Simon Peter answered and said, "You are the Christ, the son of the living God."*

*17 And Jesus answered and said unto him, "Blessed art thou, Simon*

*Bar-Jonah; for flesh and blood hath not revealed it unto thee, but my father, which is in heaven."*

*18 And I say also unto thee, thou art Peter and upon this rock I will build my church and the gates of hell shall not prevail against it.*

*19 And I will give unto thee the keys of the kingdom of heaven: and whatsoever thou bind on earth shall be bound in heaven; and whatsoever thou shall loose on earth shall be loosed in heaven".Matthew 16:15–19 KJV.*

Many of his disciples were considering the response to give their master when Jesus Christ asked who they thought he was. As they continued to ponder the question as important as that of Simon Peter, one of them received the answer to the question through Revelation from God.

He answered the question by declaring Jesus as the Christ: "Why was it only Simon Peter who had the Revelation of the Master and not the others?" We must first learn to love God above all else when we come to know him as his children. Simon Peter had a true love for his master. He did not follow him because of the miracles he expected from him. The love he had for his master and his commitment to the things of God made God reveal the personality of Jesus to Peter.

What this means is that the Holy Spirit reveals something to Peter while the remaining disciples are struggling to think out the answer. The essence of this is that we cannot be revelational worshippers if we don't walk in the spirit. We cannot walk in the flesh and claim to have a revelation about the kingdom of heaven. Such claims would be false.

I thus referred to those who worship God in spirit and truth as "revelatory worshippers. We can classify only those who are truly born-again as revelational worshippers.

We don't know born-again Christians because they speak in tongues, cast out demons, or perform signs and wonders. Even when those who work against the purpose and plan of God speak in tongues, cast out demons, etc., someone wants to doubt it; see the case of Judas Iscariot. He was among the disciples sent out by Jesus Christ. Judas spoke in tongues, cast out demons, and performed signs and wonders.

He had not stopped stealing while performing those miraculous acts as a disciple.

From the above scriptures, we also see that if we worship God through Revelation, we attract God's blessings. In verses 17–19 of the scriptures, we read Peter's Revelation of who Christ was, which brought him blessings and commendations from his master.

He was immediately promoted over others. This happens to us when we allow the spirit of God to lead us to worship him. I also want us to see the blessings Jesus pronounced on Simon Peter from another perspective.

Jesus Christ called Peter a "rock." Christ promised to build his church upon that rock, and the gates of hell will not withstand it. I think the "rock" that Christ promised to build his church on is the Revelation that Peter had, rather than the person of Peter.

Someone will agree that Simon Peter is long dead, but the church is still growing upon the "rock" [Revelation]. It is easy for the devil to hijack and manipulate church activities done in the flesh. But it is impossible for the devil to manipulate the Holy Spirit-filled believers.

I pray God will help us worship him in spirit. The spirit of God will give us the stamina we need to serve God and overcome trials and temptations.

## 3. EMOTIONAL WORSHIPPERS

It is often said that man is an emotional being. Being emotional is not bad. We should also know that there are good and bad emotions. The key thing in emotion is the purpose for which it is expressed. When Jesus visited the grave of Lazarus, he saw the people crying. He also cried to express his condolences to the family of Lazarus. Jesus Christ also expressed his emotion for the right purpose when he drove the money changers out of the temple. The purpose was also to keep the temple of God out of the reach of religious thieves.

*21 From that time forth began Jesus to shew unto his disciples, how that he must go unto Jerusalem, and suffer many things of the elders and chief priest and Scribes, and be killed, and be raised again the third day.*

*22 Then Peter took him and began to rebuke him, saying, "Be it far from you, Lord; this shall not be unto you."*

*23 But he turned and said unto Peter, "Get thee behind me, Satan; thou art an offense to me; for thou savourest not the things that are of God, but those that are of men."*

*24 Then said Jesus unto his disciples, "If any man will come after me, let him deny himself, take up his cross, and follow me."*

*25 "For whosoever will save his life shall lose it, and whosoever will lose his life for my sake shall find it."*

*26 For what is man profited, if he shall gain the whole world, and lose his own soul? Or what shall a man give in exchange for his soul? Matthew 16:21-26KJV.*

The scriptures we have read reveal the different states of individual worshippers. In the previous reading in the same Matthew 16, we saw how Peter received a revelation from God concerning the personality of Christ. Jesus was also happy with Peter for his ability to turn to the spirit of God.

After that, Jesus wanted the disciples to know what lay ahead of him. He told them plainly that the Jewish religious leaders would torture and kill him, but on the third day, he would rise again. When Peter heard of torture and death, his emotions ran wild without looking at the other content of Christ's speech.

The emotions Peter expressed are common among today's church-goers. The churchgoers are only interested in places where there are miracles, signs, and wonders. They don't want to experience any form of pain or suffering in their lives. They ask for glory without the cross. Prosperity without process is what they desire. They love religion without Christ; they are content with church rituals and traditions.

Yes, Peter did not want his master to die because he really loved him. How many Christians today love Jesus as sincerely as Peter did? The mistake Peter made, which church people are still making, is that there is no true glory without the cross.

When Jesus corrected Peter, he told him that "you are human; you don't know how God works." Our emotions do not always allow us to do the will of God.

Mind you, human emotions are subjected to satanic manipulations. We have to balance life by knowing for what purpose we express our emotions [to learn more about the three levels of worshippers, you will need to read my soon-to-be-published book, The Three Dimensions of God, Man, and Satan].

## The Laws of Growth

There are laws that guide and regulate growth. That a particular plant is tall doesn't mean it is growing or fully grown, and that another plant is short doesn't mean that it is also not growing or is stunted. It sometimes depends on the plant's species or type. Let us look at Moses.

*"In time, Moses grew up. Then he went to see his own people and watched them suffer under forced labor. He saw a Hebrew, one of his own people, being beaten by an Egyptian.*

*He looked around, and when he couldn't find anyone, he killed the Egyptians and buried their bodies in the sand. When Moses went there the next day, he saw two Hebrew men fighting. He asked the one who started the fight, "Why are you beating another Hebrew? The man asked, "Who made you our ruler and judge? Are you going to kill me like you killed the Egyptian? Then Moses was afraid and thought that everyone knew what he had done. When Pharaoh heard what Moses had done, he tried to have him killed. But Moses fled from Pharaoh and settled in the land of the Midians. "One day, while Moses was sitting by a well," Exodus 2:11–15GW*

The scripture passage mentioned above has a valuable lesson for us to take away. What we commonly refer to as "growth" frequently does not qualify in God's eyes. According to the verses above, Moses believed he had matured to the point where he could free his people from their restraints. He was mistaken. The fact that he had gained weight and height did not prove that he had reached a point where he could free his people from servitude.

Growth in age and stature is not the same thing as spiritual growth. Real growth comes when one is humble enough and has the patience and wisdom to bear with and tolerate others. Moses thought he had matured and went on a mission for which he was unqualified.

What resulted from it? He tried and failed, and he had to flee for his life.

Many men of God today have the same feelings as Moses because they lay hands on people and pray, receiving answers; they assume that they have grown up. There are no records of how some of these men became ministers of God. Most of them sprang up from somewhere and became ministers overnight. There are no records or testimonies of when there were children of God. The basic law of growth is that one must be a child before growing into an adult. There is no evidence of their childhood life in Christ.

What we are seeing are men who claim to be fully grown men of God without evidence of real growth. The process of growth requires that one be a son or child of God before becoming a man of God.

To enable you to comprehend me better, I want you to understand the foundations of spiritual growth. The transformation from child to man takes a long time.

**The Principles of Spiritual Growth: The Seed Doctrine.**

Naturally, farmers sow seeds. It is the seed that grows into a plant; the plant then bears fruit. Spiritually, Jesus Christ, our Lord, taught that as children of God or ministers of the gospel, we are seeds. For us to bear fruits that become seeds, we must first die spiritually and become plants capable of bearing many seeds.

*"I assure you and most solemnly say to you unless a grain of what falls into the earth and dies, it remains alone [just one grain, never more]. But if it dies, it produces much grain and yields a harvest. "The one who loves his life [eventually] loses it [through death], but the one who hates his life in this world [and is concerned about pleasing God] will keep it for eternal life." John12:24-25AMP*

*"Verily, verily, I say unto you, except a corn of wheat fall into the ground and die, it abides alone; but if it die, it bringeth forth much fruit. ""He that loveth his life in this world shall keep it unto eternal life." John12:24-25KJV.*

*"Listen carefully; unless a grain of wheat is buried in the ground, dead to the world, it is never more than a grain of wheat. But if it is buried, it sprouts and reproduces itself many times over. In the same way, anyone who holds on to life just as it is destroys that life. But if you let it go, reckless in your love, you will have it forever, real and eternal life". John12:24-25 MSG*

Yes, a seed must die in order to grow and bear fruit. "For a seed to die" is a spiritual statement, meaning that one needs proper training and understanding of the word of God to be fruitful in his calling and ministry.

Look at Moses, for instance. When he started his ministry in Egypt, he had no divine training; as a result, he began in error and had to abandon it. God intervened in Moses' life. He trained him to be his own minister. Moses spent forty [40] years learning from God before he was commissioned as the minister of God.

This shows that the current army of untrained, new-generation pastors performing signs and wonders is mistaken. Every child of God needs training from God and his savants who have walked with God.

Such training is not the cash-and-carry thing people are doing in the church. God's training usually takes time and involves pain and sacrifice. This is the reason most pastors, prophets, evangelists, and apostles we often see in our churches avoid such training.

The second thing to note concerning Moses is that when he started his ministry in Egypt, the people rejected him. Why was he rejected? He had no spiritual stamina to enforce the word of God. He did not have enough of the word and the knowledge of God to speak to the people, and God has not sent him yet.

One thing is to be called by God, and another is to wait on God until He trains you and then sends you. It is so sad to say this, but many people who are in ministries today have not been sent yet. Maybe God truly called them, but He has not sent them yet. And if one goes when God has not sent him yet, he is likely to mess up like Moses did.

The same thing is still happening today. Most men who parade themselves as general overseers, bishops, and church founders and try to control the destinies of people under them are spiritually unfit to do so.

The outsiders who know that have rejected many of them, even though they don't deserve any place in God's kingdom. This is the main reason some of them have resorted to alternative means of power to force their wills on their members.

Genuine growth is the kind that pleases God. Sometimes, when we see a big church with many members, we claim that the church is growing and the pastor is doing well. And when we see a small congregation with materially poor pastors, we conclude that the church is not growing. God does not see spiritual growth from a human perspective. To understand it better, let us look at some ingredients that help spiritual growth.

## 1. HUMILITY:

Humility, as an ingredient in spiritual growth, is like the root of a tree that goes downward. No tree has ever grown without roots. The interesting thing about the root is that it always goes downward, out of sight of the people.

The root is not visible; only those who want to know more about the tree would look into the root. But the tree and its root are visible to God. In order to grow according to God's pattern, we must humble ourselves.

Humility will help us go down to the level where we can absorb and assimilate from God alone. Mind you, the opposite of humility is pride and arrogance. It is pride that makes people run away from God's training. It is pride and arrogance that make you want to lead other people when you know you are spiritually empty and blind. Proud and arrogant people lack the spiritual stamina to stand up for God's calling.

*"Therefore humble yourselves under the mighty hand of God [set aside self-righteous pride], so that he may exalt you [to a place of honour in his service] at the appropriate time".1 Peter 5:6 AMP*

*"Therefore humble yourselves [demote, lower yourselves in your own*

*estimation] under the mighty hand of God, that in due time he may exalt you." 1 Peter 5:6 AMPC*

The various versions of the scripture we read above emphasised the need to go down in order to become relevant individuals in the hands of God. The lesson we learned from the root is that it is only when it goes down that it reaches the water.

Water is the source of life and nourishment for the tree. But it is the responsibility of the root to get water. If the root refuses to go down where the water is, the tendency is that the tree will not grow well. The tree will suffer from malnourishment and eventually die.

The same thing applies to us Christians. If we refuse to humble ourselves and become what the Bible says we should be, we continue to float and eat chaff as spiritual food.

God is the source of accurate knowledge and power. Humility will help us tap into him as believers. We have the stamina we need to withstand the evil winds of our enemies when we tap into them.

If we continue to allow our lives to be dominated by pride and arrogance, the possibility is that we will end up as stunted and cursed children.

We should learn from Jesus Christ, whom we claim to follow. This is what the scripture says about Christ concerning humility.

1. *Let this same attitude, purpose, and [humble] mind be in you, which was in Christ Jesus [let Him be your example in humility].*

2. *"Who, although being essentially one with God and in the form of God [possessing the fullness of the attributes which make God God], did not think this equality with God was a thing to be eagerly grasped or retained."*

3. *But he stripped himself [of all privileges and rightful dignity] so as to assume the guise of a servant [slave], in that he became like men and was born a human being.*

4. *And after he had appeared in human form, He abased and humbled*

*himself [still further] and carried his obedience to the extreme of death, even the death of the cross!*

5. *Therefore, because he stooped so low, God has highly exalted him and has freely bestowed on him the name that is above every name.*

6. *That in [at] the name of Jesus every knee should [must] bow, in heaven and on earth and under the earth.*

7. *And every tongue will [frankly and openly] confess and acknowledge that Jesus Christ is Lord, to the glory of God the Father. Philippians 2:5-11 AMPC.*

From the above scriptures, we see that when Jesus was in heaven, he had all the qualities and attributes that made him God, so he was God. And because God the Father was concerned about the state of fallen humanity, Jesus had to strip himself of his divine attributes and glory and humble himself for the will of the Father to be fulfilled.

I used to think that the highest price Jesus paid was to die on the cross. When God opened my eyes to the revelations in his word, I corrected that belief. To me, the highest price Christ paid was to humble himself before the Father in heaven. Because of his humility, Jesus came to earth to suffer a humiliating death on the cross in order to save mankind.

*"Now in the sixth month [after that], the angel Gabriel was sent from God to a town called Galilee named Nazareth. to a girl who had never been married and a virgin engaged to be married to a man named Joseph, a descendent of the house of David, and the virgin's name was Mary. And he came to her and said, "Hail, O favored one [who endured with grace]! The Lord is with you! Blessed [favored by God] are you before all other women! But when she saw him, she was greatly troubled, disturbed, and confused at what he said, and she kept circling in her mind what such a greeting might mean. And the angel said to her, "Do not be afraid, Mary, for you have found grace [free, spontaneous, absolute favor, and loving kindness] with God. And listen! You will become pregnant and give birth to a son, and you will call his name Jesus.*

*He will be great [eminent] and will be called the son of the most high; and the Lord will give to him the throne of his forefather David, and he will reign over the house of Jacob throughout the ages; and his reign there will be no end". [Isa 9:6,7; Dan. 2:44]*

*"And Mary said to the angel, "How can this be, since I have no intimacy with any man as a husband?" Luke 1:26-34 AMPC*

The scripture reveals how deeply Jesus Christ humbled himself. Through humility, he accepted to come to this world through the vessel he created. The Bible tells us to imitate Christ.

1. *Let the same attitude, purpose, and [humble] mind that were in Christ Jesus be in you [use him as an example of humility].*

   In order to serve God in a way that is acceptable to him, we need to strip ourselves of some things we claim to be our rights. We know unbelievers consider humility a weakness and stupidity in the eyes of the world []. It is through such humility that we will develop enough stamina to run the race to the end.

2. **OBEDIENCE:**

Another important ingredient we need as believers to grow and be acceptable to God is obedience. Hear what the scripture says:

*"He was humble and walked the path of obedience all the way to death—his death on the cross." Philippians 2:8 GNT*

Obedience is the ability to follow laid-down rules or instructions. Jesus did not appear in the world of his own volition. He came to fulfil the will of the father. This means that he had to follow instructions given to him by his father. He actually followed the instructions of his father, and that was the reason he was successful in his ministry.

For us to be successful in our walk with God, we must obey every instruction he gives us. I want to clarify that we don't learn obedience by reading books. Yes, you can apply one or two methods to obey orders and instructions.

Obedience is something that must be practiced. Remember that obedience is a virtue. Nobody can get it by merely reading about it in books without taking steps to practice it. Practicing obedience involves pain and sacrifice. This explains why most churchgoers cannot obey God's word. Obedience and humility are twin sisters.

One cannot be humble and disobedient at the same time. Sometimes, we hear people say they obey God. But what people see in their lives are the fruits of disobedience. As I said earlier, obedience and humility are twin sisters; you cannot separate one from the other. They are the essential ingredients for growth in the kingdom of God. Nobody can reach his full spiritual stature if he has one without the other.

Just like in plants, both taproots and fibrous roots are working for the well-being of the plant. For the well-being of the plant, if only the fibrous root is functioning well without the taproot, the well-being of the plant will be affected.

The same thing will happen if only the tap root is functioning well. To put it simply, we must balance our service and worship of God under his word. God does not accept half-hearted or half-done worship or service.

*In the days of his earthly life, Jesus offered up both [specific] petitions and [urgent] supplications [for that which he needed] with fervent crying and tears to the one who was [always] able to save him from death, and he was heard because of his reverent submission towards God [his sinlessness and his unfailing determination to do the father's will]. Although he was a son [who had never been disobedient to the father], he learned [active, special] obedience through what he suffered. Hebrews 5:7-8 AMP*

That scripture tells us that Jesus cried and shed tears. Why? Situations and things tempted him to show his obedience to God.

Jesus prayed to God for the strength to obey God, and God answered his prayers. From that scripture, we also learn that Jesus Christ learned practical obedience through his suffering. What were some things Jesus suffered? He suffered hunger, rejection, loneliness, insults, shame, and eventually death.

You can now understand what it means to obey God and do his

will. Sometimes obedience is something that must be proved for many reasons, and even God would test your obedience.

What did the Bible say about Abraham's obedience to God?

*"Now after those things, God tested [the faith and commitment of] Abraham and said to him, "Abraham!" and he answered, "Here I am." God said, "Take now your son, your only son [of promise], whom you love, Isaac, and go to the regions of Moriah, and offer him there as a burnt offering on one of the mountains of which I shall tell you." So Abraham got up early in the morning, saddled his donkey, and took two of his young men and his son Isaac with him. He split the wood for the burnt offering, and then he went to the place where God had told him. Genesis 22:1–3 AMP*

*"But the angel of the Lord called to him from heaven and said, "Abraham, Abraham!" He answered, "Here I am," the Lord said, "do not reach out [with the knife in your hand] against the boy and do nothing to [harm] him; for now I know that you fear God [with reverence and profound respect], since you have not withheld from me your son, your only son [of promise]." Genesis 22:11–12 AMP.*

God tested Abraham to prove his obedience to him, and Abraham passed God's test. As believers in Christ, there are many things that will test our resolve to obey God. Principally, the devil will test us; whether or not you want it, he will test you.

If you pass, he will not be happy but will continue to try his luck. The world will also test you. They may test you through fashion, love of money, etc. Finally, God, who called you, will test your faithfulness and commitment to him. You need to develop spiritual stamina and look to Jesus Christ for help in every situation.

*"Looking away from all that will distract us and focusing our eyes on Jesus, who is the author and perfecter of faith [the first incentive for our belief and the one who brings our faith to maturity], who for the joy [of accomplishing the goal] set before him endured the cross, disregarding the shame, and sat down at the right hand of the throne of God [revealing his deity, his authority, and the completion of his work]," Hebrews 12:2 AMP*

## Tested by Time

Time is the only factor that enables us to know if one has spiritual stamina. If one claims he loves God and is obedient to his words and instructions, it is time to prove him wrong or right.

Joseph, an excellent youth, was a good example of someone whose love, faithfulness, obedience, and loyalty to both God and man were tested by time. To get a better picture of what really happened to Joseph, I recommend that you also read the book of Psalms and not only Genesis.

1. *Moreover, he called for a famine upon the Lord: he brake the whole staff of bread.*
2. *He sent a man before them, even Joseph, who had been sold as a servant.*
3. *Whose feet they hurt with fetters: he was laid in iron.*
4. *Until the time his word came, the word of the Lord tried him.*
5. *The king sent and released him, even the ruler of the people, and let him go free. He made him Lord of his house and ruler of all his substance. Psalm 105:16–21 KJV.*
6. *He called for a famine in the Land of Canaan, cutting off its food supply.*
7. *Then he sent someone to Egypt ahead of them—Joseph, who had been sold as a slave.*
8. *They bruised his feet with fetters and placed his neck in an iron collar.*
9. *Until the time came to fulfill his dreams, the Lord tested Joseph's character.*
10. *Then Pharaoh sent for him and set him free; the ruler of the nation opened his prison door. Psalms 105:16–20 NLT.*

*"Moreover, He called for a famine upon the land [of Egypt]; he cut off every source of bread". [Gen. 41:54].*

*"He sent a man before them, even Joseph, who was sold as a servant." [Gen. 45:5; 50:20,21]*

*"His feet they hurt with fetters; he was laid in chains of iron, and his soul*

*entered into the iron, until his word [to his cruel brothers] came true, until the word of the Lord tried and tested him. ""The king sent and loosed him, even the ruler of the people, and let him go free." Psalm 105: 16-20 AMPC.*

When I first read about the story of Joseph in the book of Genesis, I never knew his feet were bruised, and they placed his neck in an iron collar. In the book of Genesis, there is little or no information about Joseph's ordeal. Much of what I knew then was that his brothers had sold him as a slave. Read it yourself for a better understanding of my explanation.

*"When Joseph's brothers saw him coming, they recognized him in the distance. As he approached, they made plans to kill him. "Here comes the dreamer!' they said. "Come on, let's kill him and throw him into one of these cisterns. We can tell our father, "A wild animal has eaten him. "Then we will see what becomes of his dreams!' When Reuben learned of their plan, he came to Joseph's aid, saying, "Let's not kill him; why should we shed any blood?' Let's just throw him into this empty cistern here in the wilderness. Then he'll die without our laying a hand on him." Reuben was secretly planning to rescue Joseph and return him to his father. So when Joseph arrived, his brothers ripped off the beautiful robe he was wearing. Then they grabbed him and threw him into the cistern. Now the cistern was empty; there was no water in it. Then, just as they were sitting down to eat, they looked up and saw a caravan of camels in the distance coming toward them. It was a group of Ishmaelite traders taking a load of gum, balm, and aromatic resin from Gilead down to Egypt. Judah said to his brothers, "What will we gain by killing our brother? We'd have to cover up the crime. Instead of hurting him, let's sell him to those Ishmaelite traders. ""After all, he is our brother, our own flesh and blood." and his brothers agreed. So when the Ishmaelites, who were Midianite traders, came by, Joseph's brothers pulled him out of the cistern and sold him to them for twenty pieces of silver. "And the traders took him to Egypt." Genesis 37:18–28 NLT*

The above passages from the book of Genesis do not give us enough details of the suffering Joseph went through. According to the Bible, Joseph developed the spiritual capacity and stamina that helped him overcome his challenges. But with the enablement of the Holy Spirit, I discovered what he went through.

*"He was seventeen years old when Jacob [his father] sent him to go and see how his brothers were faring in the field. This is the account of Jacob and his family. When Joseph was seventeen years old, he often tended his father's flocks. He worked for his half-brothers, the sons of his father's wives, Bilhah and Zilpah. But Joseph reported to his father some of the bad things his brothers were doing and how they were faring in the field. This is the account of Jacob and his family. When Joseph was seventeen years old, he often tended his father's flocks. He worked for his half-brothers, the sons of his father's wives, Bilhah and Zilpah. But Joseph reported to his father some of the bad things his brothers were doing. Genesis 37:2 NLT*

*"He was seventeen years old when his brothers sold him. Another time his age was mentioned was in Genesis 41:46. He was thirty years old when he began serving in the court of Pharaoh, the king of Egypt. And when Joseph left Pharaoh's presence, he inspected the entire land of Egypt". Genesis 41:46 NLT.*

So Joseph was thirty years old when he began to serve in the court of Pharaoh, King of Egypt, and the Bible says he was forgotten in the prison for two years.

Read this:

*"Two full years later, Pharaoh dreamed that he was standing on the bank of the Nile River. The next morning, Pharaoh was very disturbed by the dreams. So he called for all the magicians and wise men of Egypt. When Pharaoh told them his dreams, not one of them could tell him what they meant. Finally, the king's chief cupbearer spoke up: "Today, I have been reminded of my failure," he told Pharoah. "Some time ago, you were angry with the chief baker and me, and you imprisoned us in the palace of the captain of the guard. One night the chief baker and I each had a dream, and each dream had its own meaning. There was a young Hebrew man with us in the prison who*

*was a slave of the captain of the guard. "We told him our dreams, and he told us what each of our dreams meant." Genesis 41:1, 8–12 NLT.*

It is likely that Joseph arrived in Egypt at the age of seventeen. There is no record of how long he served his master before he was framed by the master's wife. There is also no record showing how long he spent in prison. Knowing basic mathematics, if we subtract 17 years from 30 years, the answer will be 13 years. What this reveals to us is that Joseph was tested, tempted, and tried for not less than thirteen years. During this period, he was able to build spiritual stamina and capacity that enabled him to forge ahead.

As you read through the pages of this book, learn from his example. Even Pharaoh, the king of Egypt, testified to his character and integrity.

Look at this:

*"And Pharaoh said unto his servants, can we find such a one as this is, a man in whom the spirit of God is?" Genesis 41:38 KJV*

As you can see, it was the testimony of the Pharaoh that gave Joseph the job in the Pharaoh's court. Pharaoh told his servants that Joseph was better than all of them because of the spirit of God that was in him, which made him have divine wisdom, an understanding of mystery, excellent character, and integrity.

Our worship and service to God should go beyond church attendance and lip service. Church leaders should not only be known for the way they dress and the positions they occupy in the church. They should be none for true love for God, faithfulness, honesty, integrity, and obedience to God's word.

### Three categories of Christians

There are basically three categories of Christians that worship God in every church or Christian denomination. These three groups show the composition of the church [the body of Christ). What determines one's category is not the level of education, wealth, or position in the church; it is the proportion of spiritual stamina one has. Add to that the spiritual ingredients of humility and obedience that one possesses.

These categories are:

1. Tested OK believers
2. None tested believers
3. Tested, not ok believers
4. TESTED OK BELIEVERS:

These are believers who have made up their minds to worship God regardless of what happens to them. In their walk with God, they encountered many things. The devil challenged their faith, and they said no to the devil.

The world came for them, and they refused to yield. God also tested their faithfulness and obedience, and they passed his test. They are true believers who are committed to the growth and expansion of the kingdom of God.

Such believers do nothing in the church for personal gain or vainness. They have only one option for being in the church, and that is to do the will of God. Examples of such people in the Bible were Joseph, Abraham, and the Apostle Paul.

All the people who were tested and approved by God had a strong character and a high level of integrity. Unlike today's believers, who value worldly things more than God's things,.

There are several things that influence Christians nowadays that make them unstable and unreliable in their service to God. One such thing is a lack of spiritual stamina to withstand temptation. Most of them act like Peter, who could not resist the influence of a young girl but denied his master when she tempted him. Read this:

*"Then they seized him and led him away and brought him to the elegant house of the [Jewish] high priest. And Peter was following at a [safe] distance. After they had kindled a fire in the middle of the courtyard and had sat down together, Peter sat among them. a servant girl. Seeing him as he sat in the firelight and looking intently at him, she said, "This man was with him too." But Peter denied it, saying, "Woman, I do not know him!' Luke 22:54–57 AMP*

*"After denying Jesus [his master], Peter went out and cried bitterly." The*

*Lord turned and looked at Peter. And Peter remembered the word of the Lord, how he had told him, "Before a rooster crows today, you will deny me three times." And he went out and wept bitterly [deeply grieved and distressed]". Luke 22:61–62 AMP.*

Peter discovered the mistake he made by denying his master, whom he loved so much. After that incident, he decided never to deny his master again. Many of us have denied Jesus Christ in different ways. We need to do what Peter did, which was to cry out to God to help us return to him.

Many believers, including ministers and pastors, have succumbed to the devil's temptation and are now under the influence and control of the evil one. They are still in the church without repentance.

Job, in his time as a true worshipper of God, was tested okay by God.

*"The Lord said to Satan, "Have you considered and reflected on my servant Job?" "For there is none like him on the earth, a blameless and upright man, one who fears God [with reverence] and abstains from and turns away from evil [because he knows God]." Job 1:8 AMP*

The Lord boasted to the devil about the qualities of Job, his servant. Note that God did not praise Job for being a prophet, general overseer, bishop, etc. Neither did he praise him for his large congregation or the number of private jets he had. Note also the phrase "a blameless and upright man," which God used to describe Job. Satan believed that Job's wealth kept him faithful to God. The devil made the same mistake as always. God allowed him to test Job by taking away his wealth and all that he had. But Job was still faithful to God. Job proved to the devil that his love for God did not depend on material or temporal things.

### 1. **None tested believers.**

This category of Christians includes those who are not committed to anything in the church or the kingdom of God. They see Christianity as their religion and have no more need than that.

They are also the group of believers who say Christianity and other religions are the same. So, their faith is that of belonging to a religion and not believing in Jesus as Lord and Saviour. People in other religions know them as moderate churchgoers whose belief in God is the same as theirs.

Satan also knows them as people who have nothing to offer God in terms of commitment and righteousness. They are middle-level believers in the church. This means that they are not fully for God and have not openly declared themselves for the devil.

The result is that the devil does not tempt them. They are unwelcome in the world because they are a part of it. God does not test people who have no personal relationship with him. Since the relationship between them and God is on the surface, God has no reason to test them. It is only faithful and committed people who are tested. God examines their faithfulness and commitment to determine how genuine they are to Him. This group of Christians makes up about 40% of the church.

### 2. Tested, not OK believers

The church's last and third categories of believers are those who have been tested and certified as not okay. It is in this category that most ministers of God fall. So many of them have been tested and found not to be okay.

As a minister, if you fail God's test, certain rights and authority will never be given to you by God. Consider the character [person] in the Bible who failed God's test.

*When Gehazi, the servant of Elisha, the man of God, said, "My master has spared this Naaman, the Aramean [Syrian], by not accepting from him what he brought.""As the Lord lives, I will run after him and get something from him." So Gehazi pursued Naaman. When Naaman saw someone running after him, he got down from the chariot to meet him and said, "Is all well?" and he said, "All is well. My master has sent me to say that just now two young men, the sons of the prophet, have come to me from the hill country of Ephraim. Please give them a talent of silver and two changes of clothes". Naaman said, "Please take two talents." And he urged him [to accept] and tied up two talents of silver in two bags with two changes of clothes and gave them to two of his servants, and they carried them in front of Gehazi. When he came to the hill, he took them from their hands and put them in the house [for safekeeping]; and he sent the men away, and they left. Then he went in and stood before his master. Elisha asked him. "Where have you been? Did my heart not go with you when the man turned from his chariot to meet you? Is it the proper time to accept money, clothing, olive orchards, vineyards, sheep, oxen, and male and female servants? Therefore, the leprosy of Naaman shall cling to you and your descendants forever". So Gehazi departed from his presence, a leper as white as snow. 2 Kings 5:20–27 AMP*

The prophetic power and anointing of Elisha would have been handed to Gehazi if he had endured the temptation of running after money and material things. The question Elisha asked Gehazi is one that many Christians, including ministers and pastors in Africa and especially in Nigeria, need to answer. This is because the level of hypocrisy and pretence among the ministers in this part of the world is too high.

We should stop pretending and give up the evil elements in our lives. Without that, we will not have enough spiritual stamina and ingredients to withstand the scenario the Apostle spoke of in the book of Timothy.

*"But understand this: In the last day's dangerous time [of great stress and trouble], there will be difficult days that will be hard to bear. For people will be lovers of self [narcissistic, self-focused], lovers of money, [impelled by greed], boastful, arrogant, revilers disobedient to parents, ungrateful, unholy and profane, [and they will be] on loving [devoid of natural human affection, calloused and inhumane], irreconcilable, malicious gossips, devoid of self-control [intemperate, immoral], brutal, haters of good, traitors, reckless, conceited, lovers of [sensual] pleasure rather than lovers of God, holding to a form of [outward] godliness [religion], although they have denied its power [for their conduct nullifies their claim of faith] "Avoid such people and keep far away from them." 2 Timothy 3:1–5 AMP*

The period the Apostle Paul spoke about is already here. All of the vices mentioned by Paul in the scripture are occurring in greater magnitude than what Paul witnessed.

*Prayers:*

1. Oh God, help me and teach me how to spend more time with you, in Jesus' name.
2. In the name of my father and my God, I free myself from everything that has been consuming my time without adding value to my life.
3. Oh, Lord, I know there are areas where I have failed the test. Lord, have mercy on me and give me the grace to return to you again, and I will not fail you again in Jesus' name.
4. Lord, help me grow deeper rather than higher, in Jesus' name.
5. Oh God, help me not to miss my time of testing, and help me not to fail you at the end of my life, in Jesus' name.

**2**

# *What's wrong with us?*

A QUESTION FOR ALL BELIEVERS, INCLUDING THE MINISTERS

I've found that we tolerate and welcome things that previous generations of believers and pastors rejected and viewed as bad.

Elisha turned down the gift and cash that Naaman had given him. But Gehazi, the God-sent servant who feeds on flesh, seized it. What's the matter with us? We now enjoy the lifestyle that the early believers shunned.

What the believers of old called "sins" are the things we have given alternative names to run away from their consequences. Funny occasions have replaced fornication. Drunkenness is called highness. Adultery is now referred to as a "sugar mummy" or "sugar daddy." They nicknamed homosexuality "freedom of choice. This generation referred to lies as smartness. What's wrong with us? The older generations of believers disciplined themselves and their children for better service to God. Today, we cannot discipline ourselves as parents, not to mention our children. The results are that there are moral lapses in our homes, the church, and the public places where we are located. The older believers had fewer options in terms of resources to serve God. Despite that, they could turn the world upside down for Christ. We, the present-day believers, are the products of their endeavors. With

35

the enormous resources at our disposal and access to modern communications systems, we are not willing to serve God as they did.

Then something must be wrong with us! As I pondered, trying to know the real problem between the older generations and us, I discovered the problem lied in the conditions of the heart. The conditions in their hearts were different from our own.

The Condition of the Heart:

We want to see how the conditions of one's heart affect his relationship with and service to God.

*"As a face is reflected in water, so the heart reflects the real person."* *Proverb 27:19NLT*

*"It is your own face that you see reflected in the water, and it is your own self that you see in your heart." Proverbs 27:19 GNT*

The scriptures above explain that somebody cannot be different from the contents of his heart. The heartbeat of the older generations of believers was to serve God and do his will.

The desire to gain money and wealth and create a class distinction in the church did not dominate their hearts. The church leaders [the apostles] and the members had some beliefs and mentalities. This resulted in people selling their houses and other properties, and they brought the money to the church. The apostles kept the larger portions of the goods to themselves because they were leaders. Rather, everyone was given what they needed at the time.

1. *All the believers were united in heart and mind. And they felt they owned nothing on their own, so they shared everything they had.*

2. *The apostles testified powerfully to the resurrection of the Lord Jesus, and God's great blessing was upon them all.*

3. *There were no needy people among them, because those who owned land or houses would sell them.*

4. *And bring the money to the apostles to give to those in need.*

5. *For instance, there was Joseph, one of the apostles nicknamed Barnabas*

*[which means "Son of Encouragement"]. He was from the tribe of Levi and came from the island of Cyprus.*

6. *He sold a field he owned and brought the money to the apostles. Acts 4 vs. 32-37 NLT.*

With the power of unity, love, purpose, and singleness of heart, the believers were able to achieve much in the scriptures we have just read. Even at that, there was a family that wanted to create class distinction, as most of us would want, but God was not happy with the contents of their hearts. As a result, God had to remove them from the church to avoid the evil influences of pursuing money and vainglory in the church..

1. *But there was a certain man named Ananias who, with his wife, Saphira, sold some property.*

2. *He brought part of the money to the apostles, claiming it was the full amount. With his wife's consent, he kept the rest.*

3. *Then Peter said, "Ananias, why have you let Satan fill your heart? You lied to the Holy Spirit, and you kept some of the money for yourself.*

4. *The property was yours to sell or not to sell, as you wished. And after selling it, the money was also yours to give away. How could you do a thing like this?"You weren't lying to us, but to God!'*

5. *As soon as Ananias heard these words, he fell to the floor and died. Everyone who heard about it was terrified.*

6. *Then some young men got up, wrapped him in a sheet, and took him out and buried him.*

7. *About three hours later, his wife came in, not knowing what had happened.*

8. *Peter asked her, "Was this the price you and your husband received for your land?"Yes," she replied, "that was the price."*

9. *And Peter said, "How could the two of you even think of conspiring to*

*test the spirit of the Lord like this? ""The young men who buried your husband are just outside the door, and they will carry you out too."*

10. *Instantly, she fell to the floor and died. When the young men came in and saw that she was dead, they carried her out and buried her beside her husband.*

11. *Great fear gripped the entire church and everyone else who heard what had happened. Acts 5:1–11 NLT.*

What factors led Ananias and Saphira to split the money in half? They were not quite receptive to the "move of the Holy Spirit." The single portion they carried into the church served as a symbolic offering to God. It also implied a haphazard approach to serving God. God demands our whole surrender to Him and our adoration. In the church today, a lot of us resemble Ananias and Saphira. We still act hypocritically and live a false life, seeming to be serving God. If we don't turn from our sins and give God the honour and position he deserves in our lives, just as it did for Ananias and Sapphira, God's wrath might befall us.

What is your heart's condition? As a Christian, what do you cherish most? We need to focus our hearts and minds entirely on the things of God if we are to restore the spiritual stamina required to finish the end-time race. As some people are currently doing, we should be aware that the church of God is not the place to flaunt material belongings. God himself will judge the things you perform and the services you provide in his kingdom. The Bible ought to shape our hearts so that they represent Christ to others. Let's read the Bible's account of the heart.

*"Create in me a clean heart, O God. "Renew a loyal spirit within me."* *Psalms 51:10 NLT*

*"I will give you a new heart and a new mind. ""I will take away your stubborn heart of stone and give you an obedient heart." Ezekiel 36:26 GNT*

*"But the Lord said to Samuel, look not on his appearance or at the height of his stature, for I have rejected him. ""For the Lord sees not as man sees;*

*for man looks at the outward appearance, but the Lord looks at the heart." 1 Samuel 16:7 AMPC*

*"Keep thy heart with all diligence, for out it are the issues of life". Proverbs 4:23 KJV*

God knows our hearts, and many people conduct their lives as if they have something to hide from God. He [God] knows every thought and intent of our hearts.

*"Don't excuse yourself by saying, "Look, we didn't know." For God under-stands all hearts, and he sees you. He who guards your soul knows you knew. He will repay all people as their actions deserve". Proverbs 24:12 NLT.*

*1. O Lord, you have examined my heart and know everything about me. 2. You know when I sit down or stand up. You know my thoughts even when I'm far away. 3. You see me when I travel and when I rest at home. You know everything I do. 4. You know what I am going to say even before I say it, Lord. 5. You go before me and follow me. 6. You place your hand of blessing on my head. 7. Such knowledge is too wonderful for me, too great for me to understand! God knows our hearts. He sees everything inside every living soul; he knows all our hidden sins, our darkest secrets, and our deepest fears. God knows our personalities, our tendencies, and our habits. He knows our silent thoughts and the prayers we are too afraid to whisper. This should simultaneously cause us great fear and great hope. We should tremble and fear such a mighty and holy God who knows how utterly wicked we are and how far removed from him we are. Also, we should rejoice and praise Him who knows our hearts. And with all this in mind, God still loves us and has made a way for us to come closer to him through Jesus Christ, our Savior.*

To reconcile us to God, Jesus Christ had to pay a heavy price. If we keep serving God with half-heartedness, he will not be pleased with us. Our hearts have doors, eyes, and voices, I've learned.

## The Eyes of the Heart

*"The Lord shall smite thee with madness, blindness, and astonishment of heart.""And then shall they grope at noonday, as the blind grope in darkness, and thou shalt not prosper in thy ways; and thou shalt be only oppressed and spoiled evermore, and no man shall save thee." Deuteronomy 28:28-29KJV.*

*"The Lord will make you lose your mind; he will strike you with blindness and confusion. You will grope about in broad daylight like someone who is blind, and you will not be able to find your way. "You will not prosper in anything you do. ""You will be constantly oppressed and robbed, and there will be no one to help you." Deuteronomy 28:28-29GNT.*

From the scripture we have seen above, God promised to deal with those who reject him and his words in three ways.

1. Madness of the heart
2. Blindness of the heart
3. Astonishment of the heart

Blindness can occur in different forms. To me, the greatest form of blindness is the blindness of the heart. This blindness of the heart is the major problem of these present-day believers.

## When the heart is blind

*"And [I pray] that the eyes of your heart [the very center and core of your being] may be enlightened [flooded with light by the Holy Spirit so that you will know and cherish the hope] [the divine guarantee, the confident expectation] to which he has called you, the riches of his glorious inheritance in the saints [God's people]." Ephesians 1:18 AMP*

The fact that the Apostle Paul prayed for the eyes of the hearts of Ephesian believers to be opened and flooded with light by the Holy Spirit shows that the heart has eyes and can be blind for certain reasons.

It is when the eyes of the heart are opened that the true

understanding of the word of God can be seen. The apostle Paul continued to pray for the enlightenment of the believers' spirits because he did not want them to lack this spiritual understanding.

1. *I keep asking that the God of our Lord Jesus Christ, the glorious Father, may give you the spirit of wisdom and Revelation so that you may know him better. 18. I pray also that the eyes of your heart may be enlightened in order that you may know the hope to which he has called you, the riches of his glorious inheritance in the saint, 19, and his incomparably great power for us who believe. That power is like the working of his mighty strength, 20. which he exerted in Christ when he raised him from the dead and seated him at his right hand in the heavenly realms, 21. far above all rule and authority, power and dominion, and every title that can be given, not only in the present age but also in the one to come. 22. And God placed all things under his feet and appointed him to be head over everything for the church, 23. Which is his body, the fullness of him who fills everything in everyway. Ephesians 1:17-23.*

Paul knew it was impossible to serve God satisfactorily if one is blind spiritually. That accounted for the reason he took it as a major responsibility to pray for the eyes of the believers of his day to be opened.

In his writings to the Corinthian church, he told them that Satan had blinded the minds of unbelievers [2 Corinthians 4:4]. Satan also wants to extend the influence of spiritual blindness to the church.

Jesus Christ confronted the religious leaders of his day, who were spiritually blind. He called them "blind leaders of the blind."

*"Leave them alone; they are blind guides [leading blind followers]. "If a blind man leads a blind man, both will fall into a pit." Matthew 15:14.*

Jesus Christ was not happy with the Pharisees and other religious leaders because of their inability to understand and obey the word of

God. They had developed into a spiritually bankrupt, legalistic, and self-centred group of hypocrites who were more focused on power and political influence than the spiritual well-being of God's people. Don't get me wrong: the religious leaders of our time are focused on prosperity, money, and wealth. I didn't say prosperity was a sin!

Like I said earlier, blindness might occur in different forms. For instance, those who are ill-equipped to lead and teach others but are doing so are blind. Also, those who are in the bondage of sin but promise others freedom from sin are blind. This group of leaders is blind to the influence of sin in their lives. The possibility is that both the leaders and the followers are doomed.

I heard a story of a young girl, about 14 years old, who was converted to Christianity in the 1950s through the activities of a missionary. The father of the girl did not want her to belong to such a religious group; he warned her to stay away from it. One day, the girl sneaked out of the house to attend the fellowship with the group. When she returned, the father ordered the guards in his house to tie her hands and legs and beat her up. She was tied to the tree and beaten severely, with wounds all over her body. By the time the father released the girl to her mother, the girl's body and clothes were soaked with her blood. She asked her mother to give her the clothes she wore to the fellowship. When she saw the clothes soaked in her own blood, she told the parents that when she got to heaven, she would narrate the story of how she had suffered a little for Christ's sake. After she had made the statement, she gave up the ghost.

The death of the girl not only made the father repent, but it also brought revival to the village. This story helps to remind us that there was something the little girl saw spiritually that others did not. She, like other believers of old, accepted to die for Christ instead of leaving to please the world and the devil. The believers of old, like the girl in the story, saw the Revelation of the kingdom of heaven. They also saw the glory above. They were able to see these things because their spiritual eyes were opened. What we see with our spiritual eyes is more real and lasting than what we see with our physical eyes. It is the blindness of the eyes of the heart that is the main problem facing today's believers.

*"Who is as blind as my own people, my servant? Who is as deaf as my messenger? "Who is as blind as my chosen people, the servants of the Lord?" Isaiah 42:19 NLT.*

## The causes of heart blindness

There are many things that cause spiritual blindness in the church. One of these is ignorance of the truth of God's word. About 85% of today's preachers are doing so in order to enrich themselves. They remove the truth from the word and give their congregations what they want to hear.

*"Preach the word of God. Be prepared, whether the timing is favorable or not. Patiently correct, rebuke, and encourage your people with good teaching. A time is coming when people will no longer listen to sound and wholesome teaching. They will follow their own desires and look for teachers who will tell them whatever their itching ears want to hear. They will reject the truth and chase after myths". 2 Timothy 4:4 NLT.*

Churchgoers who are spiritually blind will be uninterested in the truth of God's word. They would want to hear something else. The preacher would also be reluctant to preach the truth found in God's word. Rather, he would give the people the message they want to hear, and the people too would give him [the preacher] the material things and money he wants.

*"You're going to find that there will be times when people will have no stomach for solid teaching but will fill up on spiritual junk food—catchy opinions that tickle their fancy. They'll turn their backs on truth and chase mirages. "But you keep your eye on what you're doing; accept hard times along with the good; keep the message alive; do a thorough Job as God's servant." 2 Timothy 4:3-5 MSG*

This version of the Bible describes what most preachers and teachers are currently dishing out to their congregations in the form of messages as "spiritual junk food." A medical doctor once told me that there will always be diseases as long as there is junk food for people to feed on. This means that to reduce certain diseases, the production of junk food must be reduced. If this happens, it will result in losses for the companies that are producing the food, and they will not allow that to happen.

Likewise, those who are supposed to feed the church pure spiritual food are feeding it garbage. And to be spiritually alive, one needs a stream of words from God's mouth. Matt. 4:4. Nowadays, only a few of God's ministers are preaching the truth and the true gospel.

Some may see my opinion here as judgmental and may not be well pleased with me, but the truth must be told.

Why did Jesus Christ call the Pharisees blind leaders?

"Jesus shrugged it off. *"Every tree that wasn't planted by my father in heaven will be pulled up by blind men.""When a blind man leads a blind man, they both end up in the ditch."* Matthew 15:13–14 MSG

"He answered, "*Every plant that my heavenly father has not planted will be torn up by the roots. [Isa. 60:21]. Let them alone and disregard them; they are blind guides and teachers. "And if a blind man leads a blind man, both will fall into a ditch."* Matthew 15:13–14. AMPC.

The Pharisees displayed a great sense of spiritual blindness as leaders and teachers of the people. Their refusal to teach the people the truth of God's word enraged Jesus Christ as well. They were content to keep the populace in a "captivity of ignorance" in order to maintain their dominance.

**Changes in values**

Another key factor that causes spiritual blindness in the church is a change in value. Many Christians today do not know things that are valuable to their spiritual growth and development. As a result, they continue to add things that are unspiritual and irrelevant to their spiritual life. And because of a wrong perspective on the value and worth of spiritual things, some have exchanged their higher spiritual gifts and values for lower ones. Some are like Esau, who valued a plate of food more than his birth right to inheritance.

*One day, Jacob was cooking a stew. Esau came in from the field and starved. Esau said to Jacob, "Give me some of that red stew—I'm starving!" That's how he came to be called Edom [red] Jacob said, "Make me a trade: my stew for your rights as the firstborn." Esau said, "I'm starving!" "What good is a birthright if I'm dead?" Jacob said, "First swear to me." And he did it. On oath, Esau traded away his rights as the firstborn. Jacob gave him bread and a stew of lentils. He ate and drank, got up, and left. That's how Esau dismissed his rights as the firstborn son. Genesis 25:29–34, MSG*

Esau sold his birthright to Jacob for a variety of reasons. One of such reasons is that he placed little or no value on his birthright then. Second, he did not know the importance of the birthright to the fulfilment of his destiny. Lastly, he lacked self-control. Esau could not manage the problem of hunger that he had.

Many of the so-called believers of today are like Esau. They lack understanding of the word of God. They engage themselves in issues and things a believer should not, thereby selling their salvation and holiness to the devil.

So many people in the church do not love God and cannot give God true worship. The things that are most important in their hearts are the blessings and miracles they want from God.

*"These people always cause trouble. Their minds are corrupt, and they have turned their backs on the truth. To them, a show of godliness is just a way to become wealthy". Timothy 6:5 NLT*

It's evident that a large number of churchgoers are dishonest with the God they profess to worship. Their motivations for attending church diverge from God's plan for assembling his people. There are a lot of people who use the church as a place to make money.

*"Write this letter to the angel of the church in Laodicea. This is the message from the one who is the Amen—the faithful and true witness, the beginning of God's new creation: "I know all the things you do, that you are neither hot nor cold. I wish that you were one or the other! But since you are like lukewarm water, neither hot nor cold, I will spit you out of my mouth! You say,*

*"I am rich. I have everything I want. I don't need anything! And you don't realize that you are wretched and miserable and poor and blind and naked. So I advise you to buy gold from me—gold that has been purified by fire. Then you will be rich. Also buy white garments from me so you will not be ashamed by your nakedness and ointment for your eyes so you will be able to see. "I correct and discipline everyone I love, so be diligent and turn from your indifference." Revelation 3:14–19 NLT.*

The preceding scripture reveals the state of the Laodicean church. It was a type of modern Bible-believing church we have today.

The things that occupied their minds were riches, money, material possessions, and fame. They actually got all they needed. As a result, they began to boast through testimonies that they were rich and comfortable. Jesus has to caution them and tell them to refrain from folly and repent of their dead works.

Anyone who wants to build spiritual stamina for the end-time race must value the things that God values.

Sometime ago, I saw a cartoon that depicted the love and value people have for God and other things. The cartoon had two sub-topics. The first topic was, "Jesus is coming; learn how to be saved." The second was, "The Corona virus is coming; learn how to be safe." Do you know what? The second line of the Corona virus had a long line, while the first line, which asked for the salvation of human souls, was empty. This shows the love and value people have for God.

The believers of this generation must answer the same question Jesus asked the Apostle Peter.

*"So when they had finished breakfast, Jesus said to Simon Peter, "Simon, son of John, do you love me more than these others do—with total commitment and devotion?" He said to him, "Yes, Lord; you know that I love you [with a deep, personal affection, as a close friend]." Jesus said to him, "Feed my lambs." Again, she said to him a second time, "Simon, son of John, do you love me [with total commitment and devotion]?" He said to him, "Yes, Lord; you know that I love you with a deep, personal affection as a close friend." He said to*

*him the third time, "Simon, son of John, do you love me with a deep, personal affection for me, as for a close friend?" Peter was grieved that he asked him the third time, "Do you [really] love me [with a deep, personal affection, as for a close friend]?" And he said to him, "Lord, you know everything; you know that I love you "[with a deep, personal affection, as for a close friend]." Jesus said to him, "Feed my sheep." John 21:15–17 AMP*

*"When they had eaten, Jesus said to Simon Peter, Simon the son of John, "Do you love me more than these others do—with reasoning, intentional, spiritual devotion, as one loves the father? He said to him, "Yes, Lord, you know that I love you" [that I have deep, instinctive, personal affection for you as a close friend]. He said to him, "Feed my lambs. Again he said to him the second time, "Simon, son of John, do you love me [with reasoning, intentional, spiritual devotion, as one loves the father]?" " He said to him, "Yes, Lord, you know that I love you [that I have a deep, instinctive, personal affection for you as a close friend]. He said to him, "Shepherd my sheep. He said to him a third time, "Simon, son of John, do you love me [with a deep, instinctive, personal affection for me as a close friend]? Peter was grieved [saddened and hurt] that he should ask him the third time, "Do you love me? And he said to him, "Lord, you know everything; you know that I love you" [that I have a deep, instinctive personal affection for you as a close friend]. Jesus said to him, "Feed my sheep." John 21:15–17 AM, PC*

I give thanks to God for the gospel preachers of our Lord Jesus Christ. I give God praise for the Church of Jesus Christ as well. The degree of our exploits for God as preachers and Christians will depend on how much love we have for Him. We each need to respond to the following question for ourselves: "How much do I love God?"

**Our Motives**

Another factor that contributes to spiritual blindness in the church or among Christians is motive.

*"Instead, we always speak as God wants us to, because he has judged us*

*worthy to be entrusted with the good news. ""We do not try to please people but to please God, who tests our motives." I Thessalonians 2:4 GNT*

*"For we speak as messengers approved by God to be entrusted with the good news." Our purpose is to please God, not people. "He alone examines the motives of our hearts." I Thessalonians 2:4 NLT*

*"So don't make judgments about anyone ahead of time—before the Lord returns. For he will expose our darkest secrets and reveal our hidden motives. Then God will give to each one whatever praise is due". I Corinthians 4:5 NLT*

*"The Lord saw that the wickedness [depravity] of man was great on the earth, and that every imagination or intent of the thoughts of his heart were only evil continually. ""The Lord regretted that he had made mankind on earth, and he was deeply grieved in His heart." Genesis 6:5–6 AMP.*

Our worship and service to God will be determined by what drives us. Serving God is motivated for some people by their desire for fame and fortune. We have betrayed ourselves to the devil if our goals in the church are to amass wealth, fame, and fortune. One such godly minister was Judas Iscariot. Pretending to be in love with Jesus, he betrayed his master by kissing his adversaries in order to get money.

*"No sooner were the words out of his mouth than a crowd showed up, Judas, the one from the twelve, in the lead. He came right up to Jesus to kiss him. Jesus said, "Judas, you would betray the son of man with a kiss." Luke 22:47–48 MSG*

What are your motives for being an apostle, bishop, archbishop, reverend, pastor, prophet, teacher, etc.? What are your motives for what you are doing in the church today?

*"The work of each [one] will become plainly and openly known and shown for what it is; for the day [of Christ] will disclose and declare it because it will be revealed with fire, and the fire will test and critically appraise the character and worth of the work each person has done." I Corinthians 3:13 AMPC*

God will put those who serve Him and work in the church to the test when it is right. At that point, the true intentions of God's ministers and other believers will become apparent.

*But the Lord said to him, "Pay no attention to how tall and handsome he is." "I have rejected him because I do not judge as people do." "They look at the outward appearance, but I look at the heart." Samuel 16:7 GNT*

It is human for us to judge things the way we see them. But God's way of judging is always different from ours. I personally believe that "there are some bad actions with good motives and some good actions with bad motives."

My desire and prayer are that God will help us develop good motives towards his works. If our motives for serving God are not right and pure, we can't really do anything of eternal value. There are so many churches and ministers of God in this generation. But there is no reduction in the rate or level of sin in society. This is because many churches are founded for the wrong reasons. And because churches are opened for the wrong motives, they have not allowed Jesus to enter their churches.

*Look! I stand at the door and knock. If you hear my voice and open the door, I will come in, and we will share a meal together as friends. Revelation 3:20 NLT*

If it is true that Jesus is the owner of most of these churches, why is he standing outside knocking and asking for permission to go in?

Let's pray:

1. Oh, Lord, I know truly that something is wrong with me. Lord, help me find whatever's wrong with me in Jesus.
2. Lord Jesus, purge me of every evil motive in my heart, in the name of Jesus.
3. Dear Lord, please help me to reset my values in light of who you are to me in Jesus.
4. Break by fire everything in my heart that is wrong with my motives and keeping me from God in Jesus' name.

**3**

# *Understanding the power of appetite*

I want to start this chapter by attempting to define the two key-words here. These two words are appetite and power.

Within the context of this writing, appetite is a strong desire to satisfy a need or a craving, especially for food. It is also the desire for something. While power is the ability to influence, force, and control others, the drive to get something is the power of appetite.

This drive goes beyond food. It can be the drive for power, sex, wealth, or fame. It can cause great glory if the appetite is positive and backed by the power to achieve it. If it is the negative one and they back it with power or force, they can achieve great glory. If it is negative and backed by power or force to achieve it, it may cause destruction.

Let's see how Satan used the appetite in Eve to trick her into her doom.

"Now the serpent was more subtle and crafty than any living crea-ture of the field that the Lord God had made. And he [Satan] said to the woman, "Can it really be that God has said, You shall not eat from every tree of the Garden? And the woman said to the serpent, "We may eat the fruit from the tree in the garden, except the fruit from the tree that is in the middle of the garden. God has said, you shall not eat it, neither shall you touch it, lest you die. But the serpent said to the woman, "You shall not surely die. For God knows that when you eat of it, your eyes will be opened, and you will be like God, knowing the difference between good and evil, blessing and calamity. And when the woman saw that the tree was good [suitable, pleasant] for food and that it was delightful to look at and a tree to be desired in order to make one wise, she took off its fruit and ate, and she gave some also to her husband, and he ate. Then the eyes of them both were opened, and they knew that they were naked; and they sewed fig leaves together and made themselves apron like girdles". Genesis 3:1–7 AMPC.

The devil, according to the above scripture, made Eve see what was not real in the fruit he forced her to eat. She saw that the fruit was good for making her wise. The question is: Did she become wise after eating the fruit? And what kind of wisdom did she get? Lastly, if her wisdom is the right one, why was she punished by God?

**The Doors of Appetite**

Appetite is one thing the devil has used to control the world. The scripture we have just read reveals that the devil used the common sense of Eve to manipulate her. The devil used her eyes, ears, feelings, emotions, and heart to make her sin against God. These are the things I called the doors of appetite.

It would be extremely difficult, if not impossible, for one to have an appetite for anything in life without one or these doors mentioned above. When a person imagines something in his heart, hears about it, and eventually sees it with his eyes, feelings or emotions embolden him to get that thing. This is how the drive for appetite works. This is why Jesus said we should be careful of what we hear.

"Take heed therefore how ye hear: For whosoever hath, to him shall be given, and whosoever hath not from him shall be taken even that which he seemeth to have" Luke 8:18KJV.

"So be careful how you listen; for whoever has [a teachable heart], to him more [understanding] will be given, and whoever does not have [a longing for truth], even what he thinks he has will be taken away from him." Luke 8:18 AMP.

If we are not careful of what we hear, the things we hear can make us make irrational and ungodly decisions in life. It is also the same with the nations of the world. A country may say something about another country that can lead to war.

What type of appetite do you have in life? Is it a good or bad appetite? Currently, I want us to see how God, Satan, and humans use the power of appetite.

The Power of Appetite in the Hand of Satan

When people abuse the power of their appetite, it leads to doom or disaster. The devil used the power of appetite to bring all of humanity into captivity and suffering. In the book of Genesis that we have read, I noticed that the devil studied Adam and Eve very well. He discovered nothing could break their relationship and fellowship with God except their appetite. The devil manipulates them by using the four [4] doors I previously mentioned.

Satan could influence Eve to look at the fruit, see the fruit, then see the beauty and the need to eat the fruit, and the feeling of eating the fruit forced her to eat it. Through the error of Eve, a negative or sinful appetite came to dominate the entire human race. Despite the warning on every cigarette pack that "smokers are liable to die young," many people continue to smoke, which explains why. What they commonly refer to as "addiction" is actually a devil-controlled appetite channelled in the wrong direction.

**The Power of Appetite in Humans**

**Human Sexual Life:**

The rate at which people crave sex nowadays is alarming. This burning desire to have sex cuts across all age limits. The desire for sexual pleasure is also prevalent among Christians. I heard about a pastor (name withheld) who was invited to preach in another country. The story had it that, after the first night of the programme, the host pastor sent the visiting pastor some gifts. What were the gifts? He sent three ladies to the hotel where he was staying to keep him warm and ready for the next program. The visiting pastor, who was unaware of his host's plan, rejected the ladies and raised an alarm, which drew the attention of security and the hotel manager.

When the hotel manager arrived on the scene, he told the visiting pastor that it was a usual thing for that pastor to lodge his guests in the hotel and pay ladies for them.

One may ask, "Could such a church be the one for which Jesus died?" Christians who have a strong sexual appetite cannot develop the spiritual stamina needed for an end-time exploit.

Many people have died prematurely because of sexual desire. Sexual sin is on the rise today. The devil has put it in the minds of people to commit more sexual sin against God.

Now, so many people are comfortable with homosexuality. Many nations now accept homosexuality as a normal way of life, which God condemned in the Bible. They are doing it in utter disregard for the law and commandments of God.

"You shall not lie [intimately] with a male as one lies with a female; it is repulsive. You shall not have an intimate relationship with any animal to be defiled with it, nor shall a woman stand before an animal to mate with it; it is a perversion. "Do not defile yourselves by any of these things; for by all these nations, which I am casting out before you, you have become defiled. ""For the land has become defiled; therefore, I have brought its punishment upon it, and the land vomits out its inhabitants." Leviticus 18:22–25 AMP.

"Do not practice homosexuality by having sex with another man as you would with a woman. It is a detestable sin. A man must not defile himself by having sex with an animal. And a woman must not offer herself to a male animal to have intercourse with it. This is a perverse act. "Do not defile yourselves in any of these ways, for the people I am driving out before you have defiled themselves in all these ways. Because the entire land has become defiled, I am punishing the people who live there. "I will cause the land to vomit them out." Leviticus 18:22–25 NLT.

"Never have sexual intercourse with a man as with a woman. It is disgusting. Never have sexual intercourse with any animal and become unclean with it. A woman must never offer herself to an animal for sexual intercourse. It is unnatural. ,"Do not become unclean in any of these ways. Through these practices, all the nations that I am forcing out of your way have become unclean. The land has become unclean. I will punish it for its sin: "The land will vomit out those who live in it." Leviticus 18:22–25 GW.

The words of God warned humankind against homosexuality and other sex perversions. But many people rejected the word of God and chose their own lifestyles that were controlled by the devil. It is not convenient to live as a homosexual. It is dirty, hard, and abominable, yet so many people and nations want to live that way.

Something must motivate their actions, or the forces of darkness manifest themselves through their appetite. The Bible wants us to live a spiritually clean life.

"For this is the will of God, that you be sanctified [separated and set apart from sin], that you abstain and turn away from sexual immorality, that each of you know how to control his own body in holiness and honor [being available for God's purpose and separated from things profane]." I Thessalonians 4:34 AMP.

The unbelievers do not know the will of God. They engaged themselves in all forms of evil practices that the words of God forbade. What should we say of Christians and pastors who practice the same thing? According to the nations we read about in the Bible, God destroyed them because of homosexuality and sex perversions. Christians today must preach and teach against all forms of homosexuality and sexual perversion. These are the sins that defile the land. It would be inappropriate for us to fold our hands and simply observe. We should not be like the generation of Israelites who refused to serve God.

"Then Joshua, the son of Nun, the servant of God, died. He was 110 years old. "They buried him in his allotted inheritance at Timnath Heresh in the hills of Ephraim, north of Mount Gaast." Judges 2:9 MSG

"Eventually, that entire generation died and was buried. Then another generation grew up that didn't know anything of God or the work he had done for Israel'" Judges 2:10 MSG.

"And the Israelites served the Lord throughout the lifetime of Joshua and the leaders who outlived him—those who had seen all the great things the Lord had done for Israel. Joshua, son of Nun, the servant of the Lord, died at the age of 110. They buried him in the land he had been allotted at Timnath-Serah in the hill country of Ephraim, north of Mount Gaash. After that generation died, another generation grew up that did not acknowledge the Lord or remember the mighty things he had done for Israel'" Judges 2:7–10 NLT.

It is dangerous to claim to be a follower of God while doing nothing to show it. Many people may think that they are okay with just being Christians. This thinking is wrong. Idleness can make someone forget about the good works of God. In the passages we read, we saw a generation of people who were idle. They did not want to find out anything about God and his plan for them.

I want to encourage true believers to avoid idleness. You need to join hands with others to fight against sexual perversion in our generation.

Homosexuality is ruining nations and the people of the world. The devil is using some prominent leaders in the world to spread it. I want to show you the list of countries in the world that have legalised homosexuality as of the time this book was being written.

countries where gay marriage or homosexuality is legal, along with the year and country's name.

| | |
|---|---|
| 2000 - | Netherlands |
| 2003 - | Belgium |
| 2005 - | Canada |
| 2005 - | Spain |
| 2006 - | South Africa |
| 2008 - | Norway |
| 2009 - | Mexico |
| 2009 - | Sweden |
| 2010 - | Iceland |
| 2010 - | Portugal |
| 2010 - | Argentina |

2011 -        Denmark
2013 -        Uruguay
2013 -        New-Zealand
2013 -        France
2013 -        Brazil
2013-14       United Kingdom
2014 -        Luxemburg
2015 -        Finland
2015 -        Ireland
2015: United States of America
2016 -        Colombia
2017 -        Germany
2017 -        Malta

Australia is about to become a member of the group of countries that have legalised gay marriage. Several of these nations, which support homosexual marriage, have historically produced well-known gospel preachers. Among these clergy members were:

Mariah Woodworth was born in Ohio in 1844.

Evan John Roberts was born in Wales in 1878.

Charles F. Parham, born in 1873 in Muscatine, Iowa,

William J. Seymour, born 1870, was born in Centerville, Louisiana, a few miles from the Gulf of Mexico.

John G. Lake, born in 1870 in Ontario, Canada,

Smith Wigglesworth, born 1859 in Menston, Yorkshire, England

Aimee Semple McPherson was born in 1890 in Salford, Ontario, Canada.

Kathryn Kuhlman, born in Concordia, Missouri [thought to be German],

William Branham was born in Kentucky, United States of America, in 1909.

Jack Coe, born in 1918 in Oklahoma, USA,

A. Allen, born in 1911 in Arkansas, USA

Christians today are unconcerned about what happens in their countries. They only focus on themselves: money, wealth, sex, and fame. The believers of those days were conscious of their surroundings. They wanted to know why certain things were upside down in their time. As a result, they always prayed and sought God's intervention in their land. We, too, need to pray and cry to God to forgive us and intervene in our land.

"It was the first year of the reign of Darius the Mede, the son of Ahasuerus, who became king of the Babylonians. During the first year of his reign, I, Daniel, learned from the reading of the word of the Lord, as revealed to Jeremiah the prophet, that Jerusalem must lie desolate for seventy years. So I turned to the Lord God and pleaded with him in prayer and fasting. I also wore rough burlap and sprinkled myself with ashes. I prayed to the Lord, my God, and confessed. ,"O Lord, you are a great and awesome God! You always fulfill your covenant and keep your promises of unfailing love to those who love you and obey your commands. But we have sinned and done wrong. ""We have rebelled against you and scorned your commands and regulations. ""We have refused to listen to your servants, the prophets, who spoke on your authority to our kings and princes, to our ancestors, and to all the people of the land. "Land, you are on the right, but as you see, our faces are covered with shame. This is true of all of us, including the people of Judah and Jerusalem and all Israel, scattered near and far, wherever you have driven us because of our disloyalty to you. O Lord, we and our kings, princes, and ancestors are covered with shame because we have sinned against you. But the Lord, our God, is merciful and forgiving, even though we have rebelled against him. "We have not obeyed the Lord, our God, for we have not followed the instructions he gave us through his servants, the prophets." Daniel 9:1-10NLT.

The example and prayer of Daniel should be able to remind believers of their responsibility to their nations and people. If we Christians remain idle, the flood of ungodliness will sweep us away, along with others.

In his days as a Christian and preacher, John Knox once prayed, "Give me Scotland, or I die." What motivated him to pray such a prayer no longer motivates us today. Worldliness, an appetite for sex, and the pursuit of vain glory have blinded our eyes.

"But I say, anyone who even looks at a woman with lust has already committed adultery with her in his heart. So if your eye—even your good eye causes you to lust, gouge it out and throw it away. It is better for you to lose one part of your body than for your whole body to be thrown into hell" Matthew 5:28–29 NLT.

What Christ meant in that scripture is that it is wrong for someone to allow their eyes to control their feelings and emotions, sinning against God.

In a nutshell, it is preferable to avoid things, scenes, and actions that lead to sin. It is better to lose the benefits attached to such relationships and actions than gain them, sin, and go to hell.

"Don't you realize that those who do wrong will not inherit the kingdom of God? "Don't fool yourselves. ""Those who indulge in sexual sin, or who worship idols, or commit adultery, or are male prostitutes, or practice homosexuality." I Corinthians 6:9 NLT.

"Don't you know that wicked people won't inherit God's kingdom? Stop deceiving yourselves! People who continue to commit sexual sin, who worship false gods, those who commit adultery, homosexuals". I Corinthians 6:9GW.

"We shouldn't sin sexually, as some of them did. Twenty-three thousand of them died on one day"" I Corinthians 10:8 GW.

"The same thing could happen to us. We must be on guard so that we never get caught up in wanting our own way like they did. And we must not turn our religion into a circus as they did: "First the people partied, then they threw promiscuous parties—they paid for that, remember, with 23,000 deaths in one day! ""We must never try to get Christ to serve us instead of us serving him; they tried it, and God launched an epidemic of poisonous snakes. ""We must be careful not to stir up discontent; discontent destroyed them." I Corinthians 10:6–10 MSG.

There are several scriptures that reveal that sexual immorality is a serious sin and that it always attracts grave consequences from God.

It is not something to be toyed with because it can destroy an entire nation.

"While Israel was camped at Shittim [Acacia Grave], the men began to have sex with the Moabite women. It started when the women invited the men to their sex and religious worship. They ate together and then worshiped their gods. Israel ended up joining in the worship of Baal Peor. God was furious; his anger blazed out against Israel. God said to Moses, "Take all the leaders of Israel and kill them by hanging, leaving them publicly exposed, in order to turn God's anger away from Israel." Moses issued orders to the judges of Israel. "Each of you must execute the men under your jurisdiction who joined in the worship of Baal Peor." Just then, while everyone was weeping in pertinence at the entrance of the tent of the meeting, an Israelite man, flaunting his behavior in front of Moses and the whole assembly, paraded a Midianite woman into his family tent. Phinehas, son of Eleazar, the son of Aaron the priest, saw what he was doing, grabbed his spear, and followed them into the tent. With one thrust, he drove the spear through two of them—the man of Israel and the woman—right through their private parts. That stopped the plague from continuing among the people of Israel, but 24,000 had already died" Numbers 25:1–9 MSG.

Don't forget Sodom and Gomorrah. God overthrew them because of their wickedness in perverting sex. The devil is good at using people's feelings and emotions against them. He can make people commit heinous crimes by manipulating their emotions.

When we submit our hearts to God through Christ, the spirit of God then rules in our hearts. Our emotions would be subjected to the control of the spirit of God in our hearts. We are no longer controlled by what we see, hear, and feel. May God not allow the devil to use our emotions against us.

Entertainment:

Entertainment is one of the biggest industries in the world today. It is also the largest employer of labour in many countries around the world. In fact, it is the only industry that constantly employs people of all ages and statuses. It is also the single largest employer of labour in some countries. It generates so much income for individual stakeholders and governments.

Despite the good things the industry has brought, the foundation of this industry is rooted in Satan. I want you to see entertainment from a Christian perspective. Most of the things done in the entertainment industry look as if they are based on the creativity of individuals. But if one can look at it from a Christian perspective, it is more than just creativity.

The personality behind the industry is Satan. And by the word of God, we have been able to see the invisible hands of the devil in every activity of the industry. I divide the entertainment industry into three groups. In the fashion, music, and movie industries, we want to look at them individually.

**The Fashion Industry:**

This industry is concerned with the type of clothes, shoes, and makeup individuals wear at each point in time. For instance, famous people don't just wear anything. Fashion designers took care of their clothes and shoes.

Fashion designers have a responsibility to create clothing that will draw customers to them. A model needs to wear clothes that are sexy enough to draw men to her. They wear only items created specifically for the so-called celebrities. Michael Jackson tried his best to expose them a few months before he died. The average person is unaware that evil forces are influencing them to act in a demonic manner.

Let's see the origin of fashion in the Bible..

"When the woman saw that the tree looked like good food and realized what she would get out of it, she'd know everything!" She took and ate the fruit before passing it on to her husband, who also ate. Immediately, the two of them did "see what's really going on"—they saw themselves naked! They sewed fig leaves together as makeshift clothes for themselves. When they heard the sound of God strolling in the garden in the evening breeze, the man and his wife hid in the trees of the garden, hiding from God. God called to Adam, the man, and said, "Where are you?" He said, "I heard you in the garden, and I was afraid because I was naked. And I hid" God made leather clothing for Adam and his wife and dressed them". Genesis 3:6-10, 21. MSG.

The type of fashion we see in the world today is the result of disobeying God's word. It was not God's plan or purpose for humankind to wear clothes. It was when Adam and Eve sinned and became naked. They tried to cover their nakedness with fig leaves. Adam and Eve, not God, introduced this type of fashion.

I believe you must have seen the fashion, where they use pieces of material to design dresses and leave the major materials on display just to expose their body parts. That is what I call fig leaf fashion design.

God saw that the "leaves" fashion they introduced could not really cover their nakedness. God had to kill an animal, dry up the skin, and use it to make clothes for them. You should know that despite the "leaves" Adam and Eve made for themselves, they were still naked.

God's clothes were the perfect fashion for them. Later, because of sin, humanity rejected God's type of fashion and went back to the "leaves" fashion that could not cover the nakedness of Adam and Eve. Sometimes I wonder why humans love to disobey their creator.

So, in the garden before Adam and Eve were driven out, we see two types of fashion. This is A. **The man-made fashion**

(B). **God made fashion.**

As of today, it is man-made fashion that dominates the world. Satan is the one behind the reintroduction of this fashion in the world. Satan has inspired many people to create clothing and accessories that only glorify himself. He also raised many women as "models" to further his purpose on earth through fashion. The devil's fashion is to spread ungodly influence, especially among women and youth. Christians are not to take part in ungodly behavior. But unfortunately, so many Christians, especially women, are at the forefront of promoting satanic fashion. We know that this type of Christian has been blinded by the devil.

This book serves as an eye-opener and awakens their consciousness to their responsibility before God. This is important because they can transfer demonic possession through fashion. A model who is possessed by the spirit of prostitution can transfer that spirit to another woman who shares clothes with her.

In the Bible, we see how Paul transmitted the healing anointing he had through handkerchiefs [pieces of cloth]. In the same way, they can transfer demons through clothes.

"God did powerful things through Paul, things quite out of the ordinary. The word got around, and people started taking pieces of clothing—handkerchiefs and scarves and the like—that had touched Paul's skin and then touching the sick with them.,"The touch did it—they were healed and whole." Acts 19:11–12 MSG.

The current fashion "types" that are trending in the world now are the products of the evil imagination of men. So many people are content to wear the "leaf" type of clothes that do not really cover their nakedness. By exposing their bodies to others through fashion, many women refused to accept that their bodies are sensitive and should be covered. Why is it that so many women find it difficult to dress decently, even in the church of God?

"But I have this complaint against you. You are permitting that woman—that Jezebel who calls herself a prophet—to lead my servant astray. She teaches them to commit sexual sin and to eat food offered to idols. ,"I gave her time to repent, but she does not want to turn away from her immorality." Revelation 2:20–21, NLT.

The primary intention of women wearing skimpy clothing is to entice men and coerce them into engaging in unethical sexual behaviour. Contrary to popular belief, this is not typical. These women are tools that the devil is using to further his own agenda.

### 2. **The Music Industry:**

The music industry is very important. This is because most humans love music. Secondly, music is needed in every aspect of human life, even in the church.

For instance, when God answers someone's prayer and blesses him, he would come to church for thanksgiving. We usually render praise to God. That's music.

Similarly, people around the world use music for several reasons and purposes. You can see how important music is to everyone. My concern is in the area where the devil has hijacked music as an instrument of praise and worship to God for his own purposes. Many men and women have received inspiration to sing songs that can only give glory to the devil and not God, who created them.

Have you noticed that about ninety-five percent [95%] of male musicians sing about women and sex? They also used women who were virtually naked in their videos to promote immorality. And because music can influence people's actions and lifestyles, the devil has recruited many musicians to preach his own type of message to the world through music.

Most of the musicians we have nowadays are not ordinary men and women. They are men and women who have agreed with the devil to fulfil his agenda. The devil would give them wealth and fame.

Music is wonderful, but what type of music do you listen to? Remember that demon-inspired music will poison your spirit and make it difficult for you to truly worship God. We should not forget that the present music industry all over the world is controlled by the devil [chief choir master]. Have you noticed that it is easier for some Christians to sing worldly songs and music well than to sing a stanza in a Christian hymn? What do you think handles such happenings? It is the devil that is using his own type of music to lure them to himself.

### 3. **The Movie and Film Industry:**

The movie or film industry also has a dominant influence on humanity. Like the music industry, this industry appeals to the senses of sight and hearing, forcing so many people to pay undue attention to it. The devil used the power of sight and hearing, with which this industry operates, to spread his negative influence and belief systems throughout the world.

Through constant watching of certain movies or films, some individuals have changed their lifestyles to match the personalities they always see in the movies. This is the work of the devil—to buy such people over to himself. Sometimes, some movies and films shown on certain channels encourage people to go into occultism and witchcraft practices.

This is the subtle way the devil is using to convert people into his kingdom. You must be careful of the type of movie or film you watch. Your desire as a Christian should be for things that give God glory. You should also know that things that give God glory will not defile you.

**The power of appetite in the hand of God**

The only authority who knows how to harness the power of appetite is God. The motivation that propels people to reach their goals is called appetite. In all spheres of human endeavour, appetite is present. It shouldn't be restricted to just food or eating.

"But he replied, It has been written, "Man shall not live and be upheld and sustained by bread alone, but by every word that comes forth from the mouth of God." Matthew 4:4 AMPC

There are many who are eager to learn more about God. Spiritual hunger is another term for this desire to understand God better. Spiritually hungry people feel that they haven't done enough for their creator and are driven to do more. I have been thinking about the life of Enoch for a long time, and I have always pondered his character.

"When Enoch was sixty-five years old, he became the father of Methuselah. Enoch walked [in habitual fellowship] with God three hundred years after the birth of Methuselah and had other sons and daughters. So, as the days of Enoch were three hundred and sixty-five years. "And [in reverent fear and obedience], Enoch walked with God; and he was not found among men, because God took him [away to be home with him]." Genesis 5:21-24 AMP.

The story of Enoch should be able to help believers serve God better. Enoch did what people in his generation could not. He walks with and has fellowship with God every time. What enticed the people of his time had no place in his life. He only focused on pleasing God and having his will done. When God saw Enoch's determination and closeness to him, he rewarded him especially. God took Enoch alive to heaven by himself; he never experienced death.

In a nutshell, Enoch was the first person to be ruptured because of his dedication and service to God. The secret of Enoch's success was the appetite he had for the things of God. Enoch forsook everything else and cleaved to God. He did not live as long as the people of his generation did.

However, God made his son, Methuselah, the longest living person on earth. God must have given Methuselah a long life on account of his father, Enoch. Our greatest appetite should be to serve and worship God according to his will.

"You're blessed when you have worked up a good appetite for God. "He is food and drink in the best meal you will ever eat." Matthew 5:6 MSG

I like the way this version puts it. We need to work up an appetite in order to serve God in truth and spirit. This is the type of appetite we need to build spiritual stamina for the end-time race. Believers of this generation should cease their involvement in worldly affairs and awaken from any form of slumber to their responsibilities.

Some Christians are so weak that I can count them as chickens as far as spiritual things are concerned. You cannot achieve genuine success through any form of weakness. Both physical and spiritual stamina require time to build.

Look at the case of Enoch. He used 300 years to build spiritual strength and stamina that qualified him for direct entry into heaven without death.

The reason many Christians cannot build spiritual stamina is their appetite for sin. When we accept the victory Christ has given us through his death, it will not be difficult for us to build spiritual stamina to serve God.

"You are blessed when you have worked up a good appetite for God. "He is food and drink in the best meal you will ever eat." Matthew 5:6 MSG

"Blessed are those who hunger and thirst for God's approval. They will be satisfied." Matthew 5:6 GW.

"Blessed and fortunate and happy and spiritually prosperous [in that state in which the born-again child of God enjoys his favor and salvation] are those who hunger and thirst for righteousness [righteousness and right standing with God], for they shall be completely satisfied." Matthew 5:6 AMPC.

We need to develop a hunger for the things of God. No one can serve God well without the appetite to do so. It was the hunger to serve God that forced the people of old to engage themselves in things that were extraordinary for God. Without such hunger and thirst, we will continue to allow sin and worldliness to dominate us.

How strong is your hunger for God?

Let's see some people who really had an appetite for serving God. Their hunger to serve God was unquenchable compared to what we see today.

David's hunger for God

"As the heart pants and longs for the water brooks, so I pant and long for you, O God. My inner self thirsts for God, for the living God. "When shall I come and behold the face of God?" Psalm 42:1-2 AMPC

A white-laired deer drinks from the creek; I want to drink God, deep draughts of God. I'm thirsty for God to be alive. I wonder, will I ever make it—arrive and drink in God's presence? I am on a diet of tears —tears for breakfast, tears for supper. All day long, people knock at my door, pestering, "Where is this God of yours?" Psalms 42:1-3 MSG.

You can see the type of hunger David had for the things of God. He was always seeking to be in the presence of God rather than anywhere else. God himself testified about David by calling him the man after my [God's] heart.

Samuel said to Saul, "You have acted foolishly; you have not kept the commandment of the Lord your God, which he commanded you, for [if you had obeyed], the Lord would have established your kingdom over Israel forever. But now your kingdom shall not endure. The Lord has sought out for himself a man [David] after his own heart, and the Lord has appointed him as leader and ruler over his people, because you have not kept [obeyed] what the Lord commanded you. 1 Samuel 13:13–14 AMP.

**Abraham's faith and hunger to obey God**

Even God testified about Abraham.

The Lord said, "Shall I keep secret from Abraham [my friend and servant] what I am going to do, for I have known [chosen, acknowledged] him [as my own], so that he may teach and command his children and the sons of his household after him to keep the way of the Lord by doing what is righteous and just, so that the Lord may bring upon Abraham what he has promised him?" Genesis 18:17, 19 AMP.

"And he [Abram] believed in [trusted in, relied on, remained steadfast to] the Lord, and he counted it to him as righteousness [right standing with God]". [Rom. 4:3, 18-22; Gal. 3:6; James 2:23] Genesis 15:6. AMPC.

"Then Abram believed the Lord, and that faith was regarded as the basis of Abram's approval by the Lord." Genesis 15:6 GW.

"Faith led Abraham to obey when God called him to go to a place that he would receive as an inheritance. Abraham left his own country without knowing where he was going. Faith led Abraham to live as a foreigner in the country that God had promised him. He lived in tents, as did Isaac and Jacob, who received the same promise from God. Abraham was waiting for the city that God had designed and built "the city with permanent foundations." Hebrews 11:8–10 GW.

"But the messenger of the Lord called to him from heaven and said, "Abraham! Abraham!" "Yes," he answered. "Do not lay a hand on the boy," he said. Do not do anything to him. "Now I know that you fear God because you did not refuse to give me your son, your only son." Then the messenger of the Lord called to Abraham from heaven a second time and said, "I am taking an oath on my name, declares the Lord, that because you have done this and have not refused to give me your son, your only son," Genesis 22:11–12, 15–16 GW.

**Joseph's appetite to please God**

The robust appetite to please God that Joseph had made him exercise self-control when he faced great temptation in Egypt. Even Pharaoh testified that Joseph had the spirit of God in him.

Then Pharaoh said to his officials, "Isn't this the man we need? "Are we going to find anyone else who has God's spirit in him like this?" Genesis 41:38 MSG

The appetite Joseph had to please God was so great that he preferred to go to prison than to offend his creator.

So Potiphar gave Joseph complete administrative responsibility over everything he owned. With Joseph there, he didn't worry about a thing—except what kind of food to eat! Joseph was a very handsome and well-built young man, and Potiphar's wife soon began to look at him lustfully. "Come and sleep with me," she demanded. But Joseph refused. "Look," he told her, "my master trusts me with everything in his entire household. No one here has more authority than I do. He has held back nothing from me except you because you are his wife. How could I do such a wicked thing? It would be a great sin against God. Genesis 39:6-9 NLT.

The secret of Joseph's success was that he developed a robust appetite to serve God. He allowed nothing to come between him and his hunger for righteousness.

The type of life many Christians, including pastors, live now contradicts the story of Joseph we have read. They have joined the evil train of this generation, which is heading to hell. They renamed sins to be more appealing to those who want to commit them.

They referred to adultery as "sugar daddy" or "mummy."

Fornication is named "a funny occasion.

They nicknamed homosexuality "freedom of choice."

Stealing is called "smartness."

Here in Nigeria, cybercrime, network theft, and internet fraud are called "yahoo-yahoo."

This is the generation that beautifies evil things to make them acceptable. No matter what people call sin in this generation, when we commit sin, no matter the name given to it, it cannot change its consequence.

For instance, someone who steals is a thief. If you like, call it smartness. Anything other than that is incorrect. Christians should not have the same mindset as unbelievers.

Not standing up for righteousness, wherever it is found, would be a betrayal of Jesus Christ. It is also easy for many Christians to say that Judas Iscariot betrayed Jesus. But many of us today have betrayed him several times through our actions, and we are still doing it.

Rather than telling stories, we must defend our Christian faith through our actions. If we take the opportunity to serve God for granted, God will kick us out of his plan.

Personally, I would love to see Christianity practiced by Christians. As it is now, so many Christians, including pastors, are content with going to church and occupying positions in the church. We should stop engaging in empty religion that cannot help us build the spiritual stamina we need to serve God.

Prayers.

Oh God, my father, I sincerely ask you to wash my heart from every strange appetite in Jesus' name.

Lord Jesus, in your mercy, never allow my appetite to kill what you have called me to do for the sake of the kingdom, in Jesus' name.

"In Jesus' name, uproot every evil appetite and hunger planted in me by the evil one."

Oh, Lord Jesus, may my hunger for you swallow every other strange hunger and appetite in me, in Jesus' name.

Oh, Lord, I will not be one of those who only know Christianity as a religion.

Oh, my father, do not let my ears, hearts, minds, and emotions be used against me in Jesus' name.

Lord Jesus, help me, teach me, and strengthen me by the power of the Holy Spirit to build the stamina required for this end-time race in Jesus' name.

**4**

# When Satan visits you.

*"If you are the son of God, tell these stones to become loaves of bread."
Matthew 4 vs. 3 NLT).*

The devil travels the world constantly to rob, kill, and destroy people and their possessions. The devil only has this responsibility now that he has lost his heavenly glory. He rarely appears in the manner that people would anticipate. He went to see Jesus Christ in order to tempt him to sin. Christians are the target of Satan's special attention when he comes to tempt them to turn away from their faith. Every Christian has a responsibility to be on guard and to arm himself against any manifestation of Satan's presence.

We anticipate that the devil will tempt us in the same way that he tempted Jesus. But we must take note of what our master, Jesus Christ, has taught us. Instead of praying for the devil to stay away, he fasted and prayed for strength to drive him away when he did.

*Next, Jesus was taken into the wilderness by the Spirit for the test. The devil was ready to give it Jesus prepared for the test by fasting for forty days and forty nights. That left him, of course, in a state of extreme hunger, which the devil took advantage of in the first test. "Since you are God's chosen, speak the words that will turn these stones into loaves of bread." Matthew 4:1–3 MSG*

When the devil came to tempt Jesus Christ, he was unable to find

70

any means of doing so. He was forced to look at the stones he had seen in the sand. It is crucial for us to be vigilant as Christians against the devil's manipulation. This is true because the devil will always tempt someone by using what they are surrounded by. Anyone who believes they are strong without having done enough preparation is mistaken.

Judas Iscariot's case demonstrates to us that the devil can tempt and defeat anyone who is not fully equipped to deal with him. One of Jesus Christ's disciples was Judas. He began his ministry with commitment and sincerity. Like others, he actively participated in Jesus Christ's ministry after renunciating everything to follow him. He was appointed the ministry's treasurer. He oversaw the donations of cash and other resources to the ministry. He was one of the "twelve" to whom Jesus gave authority over demons and sent out to preach the kingdom of God, aside from that.

*"Jesus called the twelve apostles together and gave them power and authority over every demon and power and authority to cure diseases. He sent them to spread the message about the kingdom of God and to cure the sick".Luke 9:1-2 GW.*

Judas Iscariot used the name of Jesus to heal the sick, cast out demons, and preach the gospel. But he betrayed his master when the devil came and tempted him. The devil tempted him by using the money he cherished. Although being actively involved in God's things is beneficial, it does not imply that one is spiritually resilient enough to resist the devil's temptation.

While Judas was active in the ministry, his mind was also on how he could make money. The devil took advantage of the state of his mind to show him how to make money by betraying his master.

*"And the chief priests and the scribes were seeking how to do away with [Jesus], for they feared the people. But [then] Satan entered into Judas, called Iscariot, who was one of the twelve [apostles]. And he went away and discussed with the chief priests and captains how he might betray him and delivered him up to them. And they were delighted and pledged to give him money. So*

*he agreed [to this] and sought an opportunity to betray him to them [without an uprising] in the absence of the throng". Luke 22:2–6 AMPC*

Judas created an opening for the devil to enter his life. He abandoned his calling and concentrated on making money. That was what the devil saw in him that gave him the idea of selling his master. What Judas did is what most pastors are doing today. They have abandoned the gospel of salvation and have taken messages of prosperity, money, and fame. Judas' failure as an apostle was not because he was not anointed or had no spiritual gifts.

He had the spiritual gifts of an apostle and was anointed. When the devil tempted him, neither the anointing nor the spiritual gifts could save him. The same is true of today's exceptionally gifted and anointed ministers. Many of them have engaged in fornication, adultery, and other impure behaviours. Many members are still anointed despite struggling with various sins that other members are unaware of.

*"Now there was a day when the sons [the angels] of God came to present themselves before the Lord, and Satan [the adversary and accuser] also came among them." Job 1:6 AMPC.*

It is in the character of the devil to always go to the people to tempt, accuse, and destroy them. But we can overcome him by building enough spiritual stamina.

*"And the Lord said to Satan, "From where did you come? Then Satan answered the Lord, "from going to and fro on the earth and from walking up and down on it." Job 1:7 AMPC*

From what we see in that verse of the scripture, Satan has no destination and stays nowhere in particular. This means he has no restrictions; he is free to visit or go to anyone at any time. One may ask, "What is the devil looking for?"

Do you know that the devil had already visited Job before he went to present himself to God?

*"Then Satan answered the Lord, "Does Job [reverently] fear God for nothing? Have you not put a hedge around him and his house and all that he has on every side? "You have conferred prosperity and happiness upon him*

*through the work of his hands, and his possessions have increased in the land."*
*Job 1:9–10 AMPC.*

The answer Satan gave to God shows that he had already visited Job and his family before going to the meeting to which he was not invited. I want believers to know that even though Jesus has delivered us from the power of the devil through his death, Satan is still in the world, and you are still in the world too.

Satan is going to and fro, and as a result, we need to be very careful how we live our Christian life.

*"Be well balanced [temperate, sober of mind]; be vigilant and cautious at all times; for that enemy of yours, the devil, roams around like a lion roaring [in fierce hunger], seeking someone to seize upon and devour." I Peter 5:8 AMPC*

The devil no longer travels the globe as he once did. The devil was extremely enraged by Jesus' victory over him on the cross. Now, he's pacing the world in a furious rage. He is seeking out people, families, groups, and marriages to devour.

Knowing that the devil is wiser than men but not God is important. He can only be defeated by being in Christ and concentrating on the work of our Lord Jesus. Any attempt to veer off the path that God has set for us to follow through Christ may open the door for the devil to enter our lives.

We should not allow him any opportunity to come to us through any means. Judas Iscariot, an apostle of Christ, allowed Satan to enter him through his love for money. The devil was able to deceive him into betraying his master and getting some money from it. The devil also forced him to commit suicide, and he died, thereby ending his ministry and life shamefully.

We need to build enough spiritual stamina as children of God to resist the devil and his works of darkness. This can only be done if we remain steadfast and focus on serving God with all our minds. We should not be afraid of the devil's wanderings.

As believers, we should know that we are serving a living God, the creator of heaven and earth. This knowledge should help us serve God wholeheartedly.

*"In conclusion, be strong in the Lord [be empowered through your union with him]; draw your strength from him [that strength which his boundless might provides]." Ephesians 6:10 AMPC*

Judas Iscariot was in the ministry of Jesus for more than three years. As an apostle, he was with Christ wherever he went. When Christ taught the crowd on the mount, he was there. He was one of those who took bread and fish from Christ and distributed them to the multitudes when Christ fed 5,000 and 4,000 men, respectively.

He was in the boat when Jesus calmed the storm. He saw Jesus weep and later raise Lazarus from the dead. He was with Christ in the temple when [Christ] warned the Pharisees about the dangers of hell. He heard Jesus when he spoke of the parable of the prodigal son. He had learned that sinners could be forgiven.

He also learned how to develop faith in God through his walk with Christ. He, like the other apostles, abandoned everything to follow Christ. The question is: why did he still betray his master?

The answer to this question is simple. When Satan visited Judas, he had no spiritual strength or stamina to resist him. When Satan visits, he will make use of what he sees around you to tempt you. This is the reason we must avoid being caught unprepared by the devil. Satan visits people from time to time.

*"And when the devil had ended every [the complete cycle of] temptation, he [temporarily] left him [that is, stood off form him] until another more opportune and favourable time". Luke 4:13 AMPC.*

Another version puts it this way

*"That completed the testing. The devil retreated temporarily, lying in wait for another opportunity wait for another opportunity. Luke 4:13 MSG*

When Satan visited Jesus and tempted him, he was unable to find anything to use against him. As a result, he left for a while, hoping to have another chance to come back. What will Satan see when he comes to visit you? That is the question. Where will he look for you? In order to have the endurance for the end-time battle, you must be completely prepared. That's the purpose of this book.

*"Therefore put on God's complete armour, that you may be able to resist and stand your ground on the evil day/of danger, and, having done all [the crisis demands], to stand [firmly in your place]". Ephesians 6:13 AMPC*

Another version puts it this way:

*Be prepared. You are up against more than you can handle on your own. Take all the help you can get and every weapon God has issued, so that when it is all over but the shouting, you will still be on your feet. Ephesians 6:13 (MSG)*

While many Christians work hard for Christ, they do not stand. While some are losing ground to the devil, many have already fallen away. It was all done by Judas Iscariot. He went after Christ. He delivered gospel sermons. He could control demons. He attended Holy Communion.

He went above and beyond what many Christians would do today, but he couldn't make it to the end. Judas Iscariot tried his best, but the devil was bent on destroying him.

*"Then Satan entered into Judas Iscariot. And the chief priests and scribes were seeking how to do away with [Jesus], for they feared the people. ""But [then] Satan entered into Judas, called Iscariot, who was one of the twelve [apostles]." Luke 22:2–3 AMPC.*

When Satan first visited Judas Iscariot, he saw the love of money in him. The devil put it in the mind of Judas that he could make more money by betraying his master.

*"The devil had already put it into the heart of Judas Iscariot, Simon's son, to betray him while supper was taking place; the devil had already put the idea of betraying Jesus into the heart of Judas, son of Simon." John 13:2 GW*

The other version says:

*"The devil by now had Judas, son of Simon the Iscariot, firmly in his grip, all set for the betrayal." John 13:1-2 MSG*

Judas was already ensnared by the demon. Judas was tricked by Satan into joining the scheme of the chief priests and scribes to have Jesus Christ crucified. Judas probably thought Jesus would vanish when the chief priests came to take him into custody. He would then take off with their money after that. Isn't that witty? But the devil misled him and disappointed him.

Being an apostle and the one in control of the money meant that he was stealing without anyone else knowing, but Jesus knew. Judas never admitted that he was covertly committing sin. Despite his unresolved transgression, he took Holy Communion with others. Consequently, the devil infiltrated him and took total control of him.

*"Then after [he had taken] the bit of food, Satan entered into and took possession of [Judas]. Jesus said to him, "Whatever you are going to do, do it more swiftly than you seem to intend and make quick work of it." John 13:27 AMPC*

It will take divine intervention and spiritual fortitude to resist Satan when he comes. Do you still recall his initial trip to Eden's Garden? Please think back to that visit once more.

*"Now the serpent was more subtle and crafty than any living creature of the field that the Lord God had made. And he [Satan] said to the woman, "Can it really be that God has said, "You shall not eat from every tree of the Garden?" Genesis 3:1 AMPC*

The devil saw the woman, the trees, and the fruits while he was in the garden. He forced the woman to think critically and use logic in order to understand the advantages of consuming the fruits that God forbade them from eating.

Every time he came, the devil would tempt people by using what he saw around them. He used stones to tempt Jesus when he came to visit him in the wilderness because Christ's forty-day and forty-night fast left him hungry.

*"And he went without food for forty days and forty nights, and later he was hungry. And the tempter came and said to him, "If you are God's son, command these stones to be made into [loaves of] bread." Matthew 4:2–3 AMP*

Christ had finished his fast by then. Normally, after fasting, one must eat. The devil took advantage of that situation to tempt him by making bread out of stones.

Jesus Christ's preparation was what ultimately allowed him to defeat the devil. Peter, the apostle, was once visited by Satan, and he was unaware that the master's intervention had saved him and the others.

*Simon, Simon [Peter], Listen! Satan has asked excessively that [all of] you be given up to him. [out of the power and keeping of God] that he might sift [all of] you like grain. [Job 1:6–12; Amos 9:9] Luke 22:31 AMPC.*

This scripture reveals that Satan visited Peter and the rest of the apostles. Satan saw the seed Jesus sowed in them, and he knows what they will achieve in the future. If Christ had not prayed for Peter and the other apostles, what we see in the Acts of the Apostles would not have been possible.

Satan's visit is meant to create problems, troubles, and sorrow. The Bible tells the story of Job, who was visited by Satan and then went to meet God because of him.

*"One day, when the angels came to report to God, Satan, who was the designated accuser, came along with them. God singled out Satan and said, "What have you been up to?" Satan answered God, "Going here and there, checking things out on earth." God said to Satan, "Have you noticed my friend Job?" "There is no one quite like him—honest and true to his word, totally devoted to God, and hating evil." Satan retorted, "So do you think Job does all that out of the sheer goodness of his heart? Why, no one ever had it so good! You pamper him like a pet, make sure nothing bad ever happens to him, his family, or his possessions, and bless everything he does—he cannot lose! But what do you think would happen if you reached down and took everything that is his? He'd curse you right to your face, that is what "God replied, we will see. God ahead – do what you want with all that is his. Just don't hurt him." Then Satan left the presence of God". Job 1:6–12 MSG*

The response of Satan in this verse shows that Satan had been visiting Job to harm him but could not. Satan was not happy with the type of righteous and blessed life Job was living. He had to visit God to obtain permission to tempt Job. In spite of all that the devil did against Job, he could not get to Job.

The devil resorted to going through Job's wife to get a job. I want to believe that Satan entered Job's wife, though the Bible does not say so. But with a better understanding of those scriptures, one would agree that Satan entered her. Let's read:

*"His wife said, "still holding on to your precious integrity, are you?""Curse God and be done with it!' He told her, "You are talking like an empty-headed fool. We take the good days from God – why not also the bad days?' Not once through all this did Job sin. He said nothing against God". Job 2:9–10 MSG*

How did Job's wife discover that the "integrity issue" was the main cause of her husband's problems? Who informed her that God and Satan were competing to "curse or not"? Who then informed her that Job was maintaining his integrity? And if Job cursed God, everything would be fine? The devil spoke during the encounter between God and Satan.

*"But now stretch your hand and strike everything he has. I bet he will curse you to your face". The Lord told Satan, "Everything he has is in your power, but you must not lay a hand on him!" Then Satan left the Lord's presence". Job 1:11–12 GW*

Satan can use anything he sees to tempt and destroy people. It can be friends, family members (father, mother, uncle, etc.), neighbours, etc.

Have you noticed how the devil is attempting to wean Christians away from their Bibles in today's world? He's using gadgets like phones and other things to do this. Satan has destroyed many kids in many homes by using television. If you have the chance to read this book, you should change the way you live.

*Shake off everything that is not allowing you to serve God wholeheartedly. "Shake the dust from yourselves. Get up, captive Jerusalem. "Free yourself from the chains around your neck, captive people of Zion." Isaiah 52:2 GW*

The end-time believers need to wake up and shake off all the dust that keeps them from standing strong in today's world. So many Christians are more committed to Facebook and other social media than to their Bible.

How would they fend off the devil if he suddenly appeared to them?

You need to be aware that not everyone commits sins out of desire. For example, if the devil appears to someone who is watching a movie about love affairs, the devil will play another movie in his mind after he finishes the first. The devil will use that mental image to destroy that person.

The devil visited Jesus again; this time, he used Peter and his emotions against Christ. Remember that Jesus had prayed for Peter to be freed from his grip, and then the devil decided to use Peter against Jesus?

*"From that time on, Jesus began to inform his disciple that he had to go to Jerusalem. There he would have to suffer a Lot because of the leaders, the chief priests, and the expert in Moses' teachings. He would be killed, but on the third day, he would be brought back to life. Peter took him aside and objected to this. He said, "heaven forbid, Lord! This must never happen to you" Jesus turned and said to Peter, "Get out of my way, Satan! You are tempting me to sin. "You are not thinking the way God thinks but the way humans think."* Matthew 16:21–23 GW

Peter cherished Jesus and opposed his death. Peter was unaware of God's plan for Christ. Jesus had to die in order to atone for humankind's sin. Peter let his love for his master cloud his judgement to the point where he opposed Jesus' carrying out his incarnational purpose. Because Jesus knew Peter was serious, he had to correct him and refer to him as Satan. In other words, Jesus realised that the devil was secretly speaking to Peter through his emotions.

When the devil visited Abraham, he began to have problems with his wife. The global fight against terrorism continues today. "Terrorism" entered the world as a result of Sarah's bad advice.

*"And the angel of the Lord continued, seeing now that you are with child and shall bear a son, and you shall call his name Ishmael [God hears], because the Lord has heard and paid attention to your affliction. ""And he [Ishmael] will be as a wild ass among men; his hand will be against every man, and*

*every man's hand against him, and he will live to the east on the borders of all his kinsmen." Genesis 16:11–12 AM PC*

Abraham did not request Sarah's maid. He didn't want to use Hagar to have children. Sarah was the one who suggested to her husband that he sleep with Hagar, her maid.

*"And Sarah said to Abram, see here, the Lord has restrained me from bearing [children]. I am asking you to have intercourse with my maid. It may be that I can have children with her. And Abram listened to and heeded what Sarai said. So Sarai, Abram's wife, took Hagar, her Egyptian maid, after Abram had dwelt ten years in the land of Canaan, and gave her to her husband Abram to be his [secondary] wife. "And he had intercourse with Hagar, and she became pregnant; and when she saw that she was with child, she looked with contempt upon her mistress and despised her." Genesis 16: 2-4AMP.*

As Christians, we shouldn't follow every piece of advice that is given to us. The advice might seem great at first, but it might later have unfavourable long-term effects. On the surface, Sarah's counsel to Abraham seemed wise. That advice still has a negative impact on us today. We must never lose sight of the fact that the devil can employ anyone to further his evil goals. The devil targets Christians, and the only way to overcome him is to always be prepared to thwart his manipulation in whatever form it may take.

*"Then Jesus said to His disciples, "If anyone desires to be my disciple, let him deny himself [disregard, lose sight of, and forget himself and his own interests] and take up his cross and follow me [cleave steadfastly to me, conform wholly to my example]. In living and, if need be, in dying, also]. "For whoever is bent on saving his [temporal] life [his comfort and security here] shall lose it [eternal life], and whoever loses his life [his comfort and security here] for my sake shall find it [life everlasting]." Matthew 16:24–35 AMPC*

We need to be fully focused on Christ and his ministry's activities to win the battle against Satan. We should not attach ourselves to things that will not allow us to resist Satan. This is important because no matter the level of our dedication to God, Satan will still come to tempt us.

Our victory over him will depend on what we do when he comes and where he meets us. Our state of readiness to resist him also matters.

The devil visited Sodom and Gomorrah. He made the people sexually perverse. He made them choose the types of lifestyles that would make God destroy them. The physical environment of these cities was pleasant, but the spiritual environment was rotten. when Abraham told Lot to separate from him. Lot considered only the physical outlook of Sodom and went and lived there.

*"Isn't all this land yours also? Let separate. If you go to the left, I will go to the right.""If you go to the right, I will go to the left." Then Lot looked in the direction of Zoar as far as he could see. He saw that the whole Jordan plain was well watered like the Lord's Garden or like Egypt [This was before the Lord destroyed Sodom and Gomorrah] Lot chose the whole Jordan plain for himself. He moved toward the east. "They each went their own way." Genesis 13:9–11 GW*

Lot chose the city he thought was good, not knowing that the devil had visited the place and polluted it with the emotions of homosexuality. The whole city was indulging in the sin of homosexuality. The city Lot went to was so bad that when Abraham intervened by asking God to spare the city if he could find ten [10] righteous men in it, God could not find even ten righteous people.

*"Please don't be angry if I speak only one more time," Abraham said, "what if 10 are found there?" He answered, "I will not destroy it for the sake of the 10. When the Lord finished speaking to Abraham, he left. Abraham returned home". Genesis 18:32–33 GW*

It was actually the prayer of Abraham that saved Lot from destruction in that city. God could not see five righteous people to spare the city. There is a lesson to learn here as Christians. We should not be involved in certain things because they appear to be good. Lot was ruled by his sight rather than by his faith.

*"And Lot went up out of Zoar, and dwelt in the mountain, and his two*

*daughters with him; for he feared to dwell in Zoar; and he dwelt in a cave, he and his two daughters." Genesis 19:30 KJV*

When Lot escaped from Sodom, the next city that was close that he could run to was Zoar. He got to Zoar, but he could not stay there because of fear. He decided to relocate to the cave in the mountain. Don't forget that Lot lost all that he had in Sodom. The wealth that caused the conflict between him and Abraham also cost him his servants, his wife, and his wealth.

Where will Satan find you when he comes calling? Why do you talk so much about Satan, someone might ask? Because the world would be a paradise if Satan didn't exist, we must discuss him. Because of this, Paul wrote:

*"Lest Satan should get an advantage of us; for we are not ignorant of his devices." 2 Corinthians 2:11 KJV*

## Some devils you should know

In every battle, it is important that one finds out the strategy and the weapons his enemy will use to fight him. Sometimes people go into war blindly, relying only on their own weapons and strategies. But the best way to win a war is to first find out the strategy and weapons of the enemy. When that is done, the prosecution of the war will not be difficult.

Similarly, we need to know how the devil operates in order to fight and defeat him. This knowledge will help us gather the spiritual stamina we need to fight him on a daily basis. The devil is crafty and more advanced in knowledge than any man.

How does he operate? What tools does he use to do his work? The first type of devil you must know is yourself. That's right, you. Most people do not know that they are the real devil in their lives. This is a hard truth that should be accepted by all.

You have the capacity to do both good and evil. This truth will also enable you to grow more intimate with Jesus every day. Every day, Satan searches for individuals who he can use to further his evil agenda. Please get close to Jesus so that Satan can't take advantage of you. The story of the apostle Peter in Matthew 16:13–23 should make what I'm saying clear to you.

*"And Jesus answered and said unto him, blessed art thou Simon Bar-jona; for the flesh and blood hath not revealed it unto thee, But my father which is in heaven. And I say also unto thee, that thou art Peter, and upon this rock I will build my church; and the gate of heal shall not prevail against it. And I will give unto thee the keys of the kingdom of heaven; and whatsoever thou shalt bind on earth shall be bound in heaven and whatever thou shalt loose on earth shall be loosed in heaven. But he turned, and said unto Peter, get thee behind me, Satan; thou and an offence unto me; for thou savourest not the things that be of God, but those that be of men". Matthew 16:17–19, 23 KJV*

In the Bible verses we have read, you can see that God was the first to use Peter by revealing the personality and identity of Jesus to him. After a few hours, the devil also used him to try to stop the reason Jesus came to the world.

The truth is that the devil can use us if we are not careful, and God can use us to carry out his will. In order to avoid being manipulated by the devil, we must get closer to God through his words and prayers. Do you truly understand who you are? Do you know for certain who is utilising you? Some people only pursue fame and wealth in the ministry.

The devil is using them without their knowledge or permission. You can see in the scripture we read earlier how God used Peter, and then the devil also tried to use him. The lesson you must learn here is that no matter the anointing and dedication of someone, the devil can use him if he is not careful.

Another person the devil visited in the Bible was Gehazi, Elisha's servant. Gehazi gave Satan access to him via the spirit of greed. He lusted after money and wealth.

*"When they got to the fort on the hill, Gehazi took the gifts from the servants, stored them inside, then sent the servants back. He returned and stood before his master. Elisha said, "So what have you been up to, Gehazi?" "Nothing much," he said. Elisha said, "Didn't you know I was with you in spirit*

*when that man stepped down from his chariot to greet you? Tell me, is this a time to look after yourself, lining your pocket with gifts? ""Namaan's skin disease will now infect you and your family, with no relief in sight." Gehazi walked away, his skin flaky and white like snow". 2 Kings 5:24–27 MSG*

Gehazi made a shipwreck of his ministry because he listened to the voice of Satan that spoke to his mind. He lost the opportunity to become one of the greatest prophets that ever lived in Israel. Elisha asked Gehazi, "What have you been up to? It is the same question we all need to answer. Sometimes, we underestimate our ability to do certain things. Both God and Satan can use us. Let us try to pray for God's leading in everything we do. Immediately Gehazi saw the money and the gifts Namaan had brought to Elisha, and the devil directed his attention to them. In whatever you see, hear, and feel, don't allow the devil to use you. We need God's protection from the tricks and antics of the devil.

*"For in the time of trouble he shall hide me in his pavilion; in the secret of his tabernacle shall he hide me; he shall set me up upon a rock." Psalms 27:5 KJV*

*"For he will conceal me there when troubles come; he will hide me in his sanctuary. He will place me out of reach on a high rock". Psalms 27:5 NLT*

*"That is the only quiet, secure place in a noisy world, the perfect gateway far from the buzz of traffic." Psalms 27:5 MSG*

We can only be safe in Christ. Through our daily fellowship with him, we find both safety and salvation in Christ. We see many people in the Bible who allowed the devil to use them. Do you know that Samson was the cause of his problem, not Delilah? Do you also know that the devil monitored Jesus sometimes to see whether he would work against himself? How did I know? Check your Bible.

*"I have told you this ahead of time, before it happens, so that when it does happen, the confirmation will deepen your belief in me. I will not be talking with you much more like this because the chief of this godless world is about*

*to attack. But don't worry—he has nothing on me, no claim on me." John 14:29–30 MSG*

We should not put ourselves in a condition that will make the devil lay claim to us anyway.

## The seed in man that killed man

So many Christians always say that Delilah killed Samson. I think that opinion is wrong. Delilah or the Philistines did not kill Samson. The truth is that Samson killed himself. Samson was raised in such a manner that no army on earth could defeat him. He killed a lion with his bare hands. He also killed 3,000 Philistines with a jawbone. He lifted the gate of a city and walked over forty-six [46] miles. No human could have been able to withstand him in any form of battle.

Samson lacked self-control and personal organization. As a result, he revealed his most guarded secrets to his enemy. Samson also lacked the ability to reason deeply. This is what made him lie on the lap of a woman to be shaved. He was the one who killed himself through his mouth and actions. His life promised so much, but he delivered so little. The Bible says:

*"People ruin their lives through their own stupidity, so why does God always get blamed?" Proverb. 19:3 MSG.*

*"People ruin their lives by their own foolishness and then are angry at the Lord." Proverbs 19:3 NLT*

Nobody but you can ruin your life if you do it with your hands. Although you may blame God, your parents, or the government, you are the architect of your life. The greatest enemy you have is yourself. No Satan or witch has the power to destroy you, no matter how much they hate you. You are the only one who can kill yourself with your words and actions. If you allow yourself to be manipulated, the devil will manipulate you. Even God, in his own omnipotence, does not force decisions on people. He allows people to make decisions and bear the consequences of their choices.

When your enemies fail to kill you, they lie in wait and allow you to kill yourself—through your actions.

David was another man that the seed in him almost destroyed. Remember that Goliath, the Philistine champion, could not harm him. But adultery almost ruined him. It actually maimed some members of his household.

The Gentile nations could not stop Moses from going to the Promised Land, but the anger in him stopped him from entering it. Your greatest enemy is not outside; it is within.

When King Jeroboam stretched his hand towards the young prophet, his hand dried up. The king could not hurt him. However, his disobedience to God's word made him prey to the lion.

Several people, including the children of God, are killing themselves with what they eat and drink. Some people die of sexually transmitted diseases every year. Others blame God for the problems they have created for themselves. If you yield yourself to fornication, it will kill you physically and spiritually. Similarly, if you submit yourself to Jesus, he will save and protect you. If you don't stop the bad habit in you, the bad habit will stop you from going far and eventually kill you.

**Some other devils you must know**

The people around you are also devils to beware of. They may be your father, mother, uncles, friends, neighbours, etc. Satan can use any of these people against you. Another group of people the devil can use against you includes pastors, doctors, lawyers, etc. An example of what I am talking about is the prophet from Judah, to whom God gave specific instructions on how to carry out his assignment.

The part of the story that hurts me the most is that Satan used the same old prophet to trick the man of God from Judah; he was the one who told others that the young prophet had been killed by a lion because of his disobedience.

*"And it came to pass, as they sat at the table, that the word of the Lord came unto the prophet, and it brought him back. And he cried unto the man of God that came from Judah, saying, "Thus saith the Lord, for as much as thou hast disobeyed the mouth of the Lord and hast not kept the commandment which the Lord God commanded thee, but comest back, and hast eaten bread*

*and drunk water in this place, of which the Lord did say to thee, "Eat no bread and drink no water," thy carcass shall not come unto the sepulture of thy fathers. And it came to pass, after he had eaten bread, and after he had drunk, that he saddled for him the ass, to wit, for the prophet whom he had brought back. And when he has gone, a lion met him by the way, and slew him; and his carcass was cast in the way, and the ass stood by it, the lion also stood by the carcass. And, behold, men passed by and saw the carcass cast in the way and the lion standing by the carcass; and they came and told it in the city where the old prophet dwelt. And when the prophet that brought him back form the way heard thereof, he said, it is the man of God, who was disobedient with the word of the Lord. Therefore the Lord has delivered him to the lion, which has torn him and slain him, according to the word of the Lord, which he spoke to him". 1 Kings 13:20–26 KJV*

In that story, the old prophet deceived the young prophet by lying. There is a need for us to be careful about how we live our lives. Satan can use anyone against you. Whenever Satan visits, you run to Jesus Christ. He is the only true pillar of safety.

*"Neither is there salvation in any other; for there is none other name under heaven given among men, whereby we must be saved". Acts 4:12 KJV*

It is only through Christ that we can be delivered from the onslaught and assault of the devil that come to us as temptations. Note that some of the temptations of Satan come as blessings and are capable of deceiving people, while others are packages of direct destruction.

**The soul traders**

*"What kind of deal is it to get everything you want but lose yourself? ""What could you ever trade your soul for?" Matthew 16:26 MSG*

*"For what will it profit a man if he gains the whole world and forfeits his life [his blessed life in the kingdom of God]? Or what would a man give as an exchange for his blessed life [in the kingdom of God]?" Matthew 16:20 AMPC*

Both versions of the Bible talk about the same thing but explain it with various words for better understanding. The first version says, "What kind of deal is it to gain everything and lose the most important thing? Your soul. While the second version says, "What are you giving in exchange for your soul? We should know that Satan is an expert at negotiating and buying off the souls of men. It is an act of foolishness to engage Satan in any form of transaction. No one has ever bargained with the devil and won him. Satan always has a way of making people lose whenever they trade with him.

Jesus Christ has already given his life in exchange for ours. We need to stick close to Christ to avoid being tricked by Satan. I was told the story of an unemployed graduate prayer warrior in a certain church. He was an effective prayer warrior, whose prayers hindered the activities of an occultist who lived in the same building as him. The occult man had tried to stop the young man from praying but could not. Then he discovered that the prayer warrior was a graduate and also unemployed.

The occult man introduced the young man to somebody who gave him a job with a fabulous salary and allowances. God revealed to another brother in the church that the prayer warrior's life was to be cut short by two men. But he rejected the Revelation; rather, he claimed that enemies were after his blessings.

The devil used Job to trap him out of his prayer life and service to God. Although he supported the church's programmes with money, his relationship with God was tampered with. After two years and seven months on the Job, he died suddenly, bringing to fulfilment the Revelation a brother had about him. What happened to him was that the devil traded away his prayer life for the job he got.

This is what I call a "soul trader. The young man gave testimony in the church and praised God for answering his prayer. But in a real sense, God was not involved in the whole thing. It was the arrangement of the devil to rob him of his fruitful spiritual life in exchange for Job. Sometimes, some of the things or blessings we claim God gives us have a disclaimer from God. It is only someone with strong spiritual insight who can see such a disclaimer notice. I want to believe the prophet Elisha saw the disclaimer notice on the gifts Namaan brought to him, but Gehazi did not see it.

*But Elisha replied, "As surely as the Lord lives, whom I serve, I will not accept any gifts. And though Naaman urged him to take the gift, Elisha refused. Then Naaman said, "All right, but please allow me to load two of my mules with earth from this place, and I will take it back home with me. From now on, I will never again offer burnt offerings or sacrifices to any other God except the Lord. However, may the Lord pardon me for this one thing. When my master the king goes into the temple of the God Rimmon to worship there and lean my arm, may the Lord pardon me when I bow, too. ""Go in peace," Elisha said. So Naaman started home again.  But Gehazi, the servant of Elisha, the man of God, said to himself, "my master should not have let this Aramean get away without accepting any of his gifts. ""As surely as the Lord lives, I will chase after him and get something from him." "So Gehazi set off after Naaman, and when Naaman saw Gehazi running after him, he climbed down from his chariot and went to meet him." Is everything all right? Naaman asked, "Yes," Gehazi said, "but my master has sent me to tell you that two young prophets from the hill country of Ephraim have just arrived. He would like to give them 75 pounds of silver and two sets of clothing.*

*"By all means, take twice as much silver," Naaman insisted. He gave him two sets of clothing, tied up the money in two bags, and sent two of his servants to carry the gifts for Gehazi, but when they arrived at the citadel, Gehazi took the gifts from the servants and sent the men back. Then he went and hid the gifts inside the house. When he went in to see his master, Elisha asked, "Where have you been, "Gehazi?" "I have not been anywhere," he replied. But Elisha asked him, "Don't you realize that I was there in spirit when Naaman stepped down from his chariot to meet you?" "Is this the time to receive money and clothing, olive groves and vineyards, sheep and cattle, and male and female servants? ""Because you have done this, you and your descendants will suffer from Naaman's leprosy forever." When Gehazi left the room, he was covered with leprosy; his skin was as white as snow. 2 Kings 5:16–27 NLT.*

We should always pray that anything the devil wants to use to distract and derail us from God's purpose and plan may never see the light of day. Sometimes, God does not answer certain prayers the way we want them answered because he does not want us to go astray. We also need to reexamine ourselves to see if we are really in Christ. We should also find out whether the job or business we are doing is from God! You should know that no amount of tithes and offerings can take the place of your prayers and fellowship with God.

Even if you build a church for God and sponsor other church projects, but your prayer life and fellowship with God are zero, you have lost all. Business and jobs are no sin, but they should not become a bargain for your soul.

When a Christian woman has sex with someone else in order to get a job or gain promotion at work, it amounts to "soul trading. The way many things appear in the physical eyes is not like that in the spiritual eyes.

*"And he said to them, guard yourselves and keep free from all covetousness [the immoderate desire for wealth and the greedy longing to have more], for a man's life does not consist in and is not derived from possessing overflowing abundance or that which is over and above his needs." Luke 12:15 AMPC*

I used to marvel at why, despite everything that had occurred to him, Job did not have high blood pressure. When Satan came to visit Job, he ruined all he owned and then gave him boils. What kept Job believing in God despite all of his difficulties?

*"One day the members of the heavenly court came to present themselves before the Lord, and the accuser, Satan, came with them, asking, "Where have you come from?" The Lord asked Satan. Satan answered the Lord, "I have been patrolling the earth, watching everything that is going on." Then the Lord asked Satan, "Have you noticed my servant Job? He is the finest man in all the earth. He is blameless—a man of complete integrity. He fears God and stays away from evil". Satan replied to the Lord, "Yes," but Job has good reason to fear God. You have always put a wall of protection around him, his home, and his property. You have made him prosper in everything he does. "Look how rich he is!" "But reach out and take away everything he has, and he will*

*surely curse you to your face." "All right, you may test him," the Lord said to Satan. "Do whatever you want with everything he possesses, but don't harm him physically." So Satan left the Lord's presence. One day, when Job's sons and daughter were feasting at the house of the oldest brother, a messenger arrived at Job's home with this news:"Your oxen were plowing, with the donkeys feeding beside them, when the Sabeans raided us. They stole all the animals and killed all the farmhands. I am the only one who escaped to tell you. "While he was still speaking, another messenger arrived with this news. The fire of God has fallen from heaven and burned up your sheep and all the shepherds. "I am the only one who escaped to tell you." While he was still speaking, a third messenger arrived with this news. "Three bands of Chaldean raiders have stolen your camels and killed your servants. I am the only one who escaped to tell you. While he was still speaking, another messenger arrived with this news. "Your sons and daughters were feasting in their oldest brother's home when, suddenly, a powerful wind swept in from the wilderness and hit the house on all sides. The house collapsed, and all your children are dead. "I am the only one who escaped to tell you." Job stood up and tore his robe in grief. There, he shaved his head and fell to the ground to worship. He said, "I came naked from my mother's womb, and I will be naked when I leave. The Lord gave me what I had, and the Lord has taken it away. Praise the name of the Lord!" In all of this, Job did not sin by blaming God". Job 1:6-22 NLT.*

Job's story is amazing in the sense that most Christians would have died the same day the first incident happened to them. The Holy Spirit made me understand that Job did not allow anything to control his heart. Job's focus in life was to please God.

Unlike many pastors and believers of today, who believe their lives depend on what they have, so many pastors don't pray for everybody. It is only the rich and highly placed people that they pray for. Certain seats and positions in so many churches are reserved for certain individuals. The messages of the pastors are on prosperity, money, and fame. Get me right! Prosperity is good, but without the salvation of the soul, prosperity will amount to fruitless labor. Satan has visited many pastors and churches without their knowledge. The main mission of such a visit is always to exchange something for something else.

1. *During that time, the devil came and said to him, "If you are the son of God, tell these stones to become loaves of bread."*
2. *But Jesus told him, "No! The scriptures say, "People do not live by bread alone, but by every word that comes from the mouth of God." Matthew 4:3–4 NLT.*

Mark the phrase "the devil came." He came for what? to negotiate and bargain for something. Satan started his business by asking Christ to turn stones into bread. This bargain was an exchange of priorities. Satan knew that Jesus had the power to do it. He wanted Jesus to exchange the word of God, which is the bread of life, with the physical bread. How did I know? The answer is in the response Jesus gave Satan: "Man shall not live by bread alone." Talking about physical bread [food], but by every word of God. Jesus looked beyond Satan's request and went into the motive of Satan's bargain.

Jesus saw that the motive behind the request was a "show of power." As a bargain for an exchange of priorities, my prayer is that we should be able to see beyond what is always presented before us.

1. *Then the devil took him to the Holy City, Jerusalem, to the highest point of the tempest, 6 And he said, "If you are a son of God, jump off! For the Scriptures say: "He will order his angels to protect you." "And they will hold you up with their hands so you won't even hurt your foot on a stone." 7. Jesus responded, "The scriptures also say, "You must not test the Lord your God." Matthew 4:5-7 NLT*

The next temptation of Satan was the bargain to exchange faith for doubt. Satan took Jesus to the pinnacle of the temple, a place of faith. He did not take Jesus somewhere else. Why? Satan knew Jesus was the son of God. He heard it when John the Baptist called him the Lamb of

God. Satan saw when heaven opened and the Holy Spirit came upon Jesus, and a voice from heaven said, "This is my beloved son, in whom I am well pleased." He knew all these facts about Jesus, but still went ahead and said to him, "If you are the son of God, what was he trying to achieve? The answer is simple. The devil wanted to cast doubt on the life of Jesus. He tried to make Jesus "show off his power." The truth is that doubt always follows a show of power. The devil also wanted Jesus to obey him by casting himself down. This would mean Jesus doubting himself and the word of God.

Jesus knew he was the son of God, and he did not need to prove it to the devil. By quoting the scriptures to support his request for Jesus to jump off, the devil wanted Jesus to doubt the word of God. Note that Jesus was always looking for the motive behind what the devil requested. Jesus told Satan not to tempt God.

To tempt God means you are doubting him. If you are sure of the word of God, you don't need to test it again. The idea of testing something is to find out whether it is good, correct, or authentic.

1. *Next, the devil took him to the peak of a very high mountain and showed him all the kingdoms of the world and their glory. 9. "I will give it all to you," he said, "if you will kneel down and worship me."*

2. *"Get out of here, Satan," Jesus told him, "for the scriptures say that you must worship the Lord your God and serve only him." 11. Then the devil went away, and angels came and took care of Jesus. Matthew 4:8–11 NLT.*

This was the most serious and greatest of all the temptations that Jesus went through. Satan wanted Jesus to exchange his glory as a creator of all things, with him [Satan] as a creature, for things Jesus created by himself. Jesus did not waste time with Satan. Jesus commanded him to get lost. The devil obeyed and left him. Satan has trapped so many Christians with this bargain.

Take time to check on some of the blessings that come to you to see whether they are from God or Satan. When Satan comes to you for a bargain, be strong and bold enough to challenge him to get behind you.

Prayers:

- Dear Lord, now that I know Satan is still very much around and that he is looking for ways to get me, Lord Jesus, I hide myself in you; I hide myself thoroughly in you in Jesus' name.
- Lord, I receive the grace, the power, and the authority in Jesus' name to stand against any satanic visitation in my life.
- Oh, Lord, my God, I know I can't pray out temptation from my life, but I pray for the strength to withstand any temptation and overcome it as Jesus did, in Jesus' name.
- Oh God, my Lord, cast your fire in my heart and soul. I refuse to trade my soul for anything in this world, and I break any power bargaining for my soul in Jesus name.
- Any evil seed in me assigned to kill me, I break and destroy in Jesus' name.

# 5

# Delicious Poison.

Daniel 1 vs. 3:16

*"But Daniel purposed in his heart that he would not defile himself with the portion of the king's meat nor with the wine that he drank; therefore he requested of the prince of the Eunochs that he might not defile himself." Daniel 1:8 KJV*

*"Daniel made up his mind not to harm himself by eating the king's rich food and drinking the king's wine. So he asked the chief of staff for permission not to harm himself in this way." Daniel 1:8 GW*

Poison, within the context of this book, is anything edible or not that can pollute, damage, contaminate, and defile someone physically and spiritually. Ordinarily, it is not common for people to see poisonous food and drink, and they still eat it.

People can only eat poisonous food if they are deceived or are not aware that the food has been poisoned. If someone is deceived into eating poison, the person who prepares the food has to do it in the most delicious manner to attract his victim.

By so doing, the person who is about to be poisoned would not know that the food has been poisoned.

Probably, it will be after he has eaten the food and is dead that some other people will find out that the man died of food poisoning. In

Daniel's case, he feared succumbing to spiritual poison. This does not imply that the food the king served them contained any sort of actual poison. No, it didn't. Daniel believed that a heathen king's food must have been sacrificed to the idols that he worshipped.

And eating the same food with the king would amount to worshipping the idols of the king. Daniel tried to avoid such spiritual poison and, as a result, requested common food.

Daniel and his three companions considered the king's food to be delicious poison, despite the fact that it was an honour to eat the same food as him. Don't forget that other people also had the chance to partake in the king's cuisine, just as Daniel and his friends did.

Daniel believed that the delectable poison in the food had the power to put an end to their spiritual life. Additionally, it was wrong; eating the food of the gentile king was a sin against God.

As Christians, we ought to be able to evaluate some of the opportunities that present themselves and determine whether or not they are truly from God. Many Christians have consumed delicious poison as a result of getting married, starting a business, getting a job in ministry, etc.

They were deceived by the devil because those delicious poisons were packaged in beautiful forms. Some of the things people are collecting as gifts and blessings, some of which may even be from the devil, are packaged as letter bombs for them. They are dead by the time they open the package and want to see what's inside.

Daniel and his friends were not carried away by the opportunity to serve the king. They were more concerned with their relationship and fellowship with God.

A young man asked his grandfather how his generation was able to live without technology, the internet, air conditioners, mobile phones, Facebook, etc.

The grandfather replied, saying that my generation was able to live without those things just as the generation of the young man is able to live without prayers, honour, compassion, respect, love, shame, honesty, and modesty.

To me, it appears people who were born between 1950 and 1986 are more blessed in terms of morals than those born after that period of time. During that period of time, most of the social infrastructure and social media were not available.

But people were able to relate intimately, and the level of trust and understanding was very high.

*"This is what the Lord says; stand at the crossroads and look. Ask which paths are the old, reliable ones. Ask which way leads to blessings. Live that way, and find a resting place for yourselves. But you said that you would not do it that way. Jeremiah 6:16 NLT.*

*"Go stand at the crossroads and look around. Ask for direction so to the old road, the tried and true road. Then take it. Discover the right route to your soul. But they said, "Nothing doing. We are not going that way. I even provided watchmen for them to warn them and set off the alarm. But the people said it was a false alarm. It does not concern us. And so I am calling in the nations as witnesses: "Watch, witnesses, what happens to them! And pay attention, Earth! Don't miss these bulletins. I am writing a catastrophe about these people, the end result of the games they have been playing with me. They have ignored everything I have said and had nothing but contempt for my teaching. What would I want with incense brought in from Sheba and rare spices from exotic places? Your burnt sacrifices in worship give me no pleasure. "Your religious rituals mean nothing to me." Jeremiah 6:16–20 MSG.*

The reason for using various versions of the Bible is to bring greater understanding to what I am saying. Don't forget, we are still on the spiritual stamina track for the end-time Christian.

**components of man.**

Man is a triune creature, made up of body, soul, and spirit.

*"Now may the God of peace himself sanctify you through and through [that is, separate you from profane and vulgar things, make you pure and whole and undamaged, consecrated to him—set apart for his purpose]; and may your spirit, soul, and body be kept complete and [be found] blameless at the coming of our Lord Jesus Christ." I Thessalonians 5:23 AMP.*

*"May the God who gives peace make you holy in every way." "May he keep your whole being—spirit, soul, and body—blameless when our Lord Jesus comes." I Thessalonians 5:23 GW*

*"God's word is living and active. It is sharper than any two-edged sword and cuts as deep as the place where soul and spirit meet, the place where joints and marrow meet. God's word judges a person's thoughts and intentions".Hebrews 4:12 (GW)*

*"Don't be bluffed into silence by the threats of bullies. ""There is nothing they can do to your soul, your core being, save your fear for God, who holds your entire life—body and soul—in his hands." Matthew 10:28 MSG.*

All the scriptures above justify what I am saying. You need to know this truth and hold fast to it. It is the mouth that feeds the body. The heart feeds the spirit. The soul feeds through the eyes and ears. When the eyes and ears feed the soul, the soul passes the information to the heart, which in turn feeds the spirit. This is the reason the Bible says:

*"Keep a vigilant watch over your heart; that is where life starts. ""Keep your eyes straight ahead; ignore all sideshow distractions. ""Watch your step, and the road will stretch out smoothly before you. ""Look neither right nor left; leave evil in the dust." Proverb 4:23, 25–27 MSG*

*"Guard your heart more than anything else, because the source of your life flows from it. Let your eyes look straight ahead, and your sight be focused in front of you. Carefully walk a straight path, and all your ways will be secured. "Do not lean to the right or to the left; walk away from evil." Proverb 4:23, 25–27 GW*

Jesus Christ also said:

*"Blessed are the pure in heart, for they shall see God." Matthew 5:8 KJV*

*"Blessed [those who anticipate God's presence and are spiritually mature] are the pure in heart [those with integrity, moral courage, and godly character], for they will see God." Matthew 5:8 AMP*

*"Who shall ascend into the hill of the Lord? Or who shall stand in his holy*

*place? He that hath clean hands, and a pure heart; who hath lifted up his soul unto vanity, nor sworn deceitfully". Psalms 24:3–4 KJV*

You must be familiar with the parts of a person and how they function. Really, what you feed yourself matters. The heart transmits what you feed your soul to your spirit, who then receives it. What you eat will determine whether you are spiritually alive or dead.

Both positive and negative things can enter the feeding channels. You have the right to eat whatever you want, just as the mouth has the ability to take in both healthy food that provides nutrients for the body and poison that can kill it. "I won't pollute myself with the king's meat," Daniel declared. When King David realised that his heart was consuming spiritual junk food, he too sobbed.

*"Soak me in your laundry, and I will come out clean; scrub me, and I will have a snow white life." Psalms 51:7 MSG.*

*"Create in me a clean heart, O God, and renew a right and steadfast spirit within me." Psalms 51:10 AMP.*

Most of the things people clamour for in this generation are actually poison to the soul and spirit of man. The invention of those things had many advantages, and that led to a serious transformation worldwide.

But as Christians, we must be honest and say that these inventions have more drawbacks than benefits. Technology, the internet, computers, television, mobile phones, and other inventions are a few of them. Some of these innovations have simplified modern life. Modern life would be very challenging without them.

The gospel was thriving without microphones and public address systems before technology was created. The gospel was powerfully preached by the old ministers, who forced sinners to turn from their ways. I occasionally ponder why something they created to improve life has turned out to be detrimental to it.

Peter the Apostle converted three thousand men to Christ in a single sermon given without a microphone. The home of John the Baptist was in a wilderness area. The entire city of Jerusalem turned out to hear his message, despite the fact that there was no radio, television, or handbill advertising his programmes.

*"In those days came John the Baptist, preaching in the wilderness of Judea, and saying, "Repent, for the kingdom of heaven is at hand. For this is he who was spoken of by the prophet Esaias, saying, "The voice of one crying in the wilderness says: Prepare the way of the Lord; make his paths straight. And the same John had his raiment of camel's hair and a leather girdle about his loins, and his meat was locusts and wild honey. Then went out to him, Jerusalem and all Judea, and all the region round about Jordan, and were baptized of him in Jordan, confessing their sins". Matthew 3:1–6 KJA.*

How did these men achieve so much without technology? How were they able to gather so many people without technology? I don't mean to imply that technology is sinful or bad, but there are some instances in which it could be a lethal weapon in the hands of the devil. He'll also use it as poison, for instance, to kill believers' spirits. Many Christians are losing track of their Bibles because of Facebook.

*"Then the Lord spoke to Jonah a second time:"Get up and go to the great city of Nineveh and deliver the message I have given you." This time Jonah obeyed the Lord's command and went to Nineveh, a city so large that it took three days to see it all. On the day Jonah entered the city, he shouted to the crowds. "Forty days from now, Nineveh will be destroyed." The people of Nineveh believed God's message, and from the greatest to the least, they declared a fast and put on burlap to show their sorrow. When the king of Nineveh heard what Jonah was saying, he stepped down from his throne and took off his royal robes. He dressed himself in burlap and sat on a heap of ashes. Then the king and his nobles sent this decree throughout the city. "No one, not even the animals from your herds and flocks, may eat or drink anything at all. People and animals alike must wear garments of mourning, and everyone must pray earnestly to God. They must turn from their evil ways and stop all their violence. Who can tell? Perhaps even now, God will change his mind and hold back his fierce anger from destroying us. When God saw what they had done and how they*

*had put a stop to their evil ways, he changed his mind and did not carry out the destruction he had threatened". Jonah 3:1–10 NLT.*

In this generation, technology is doing us more harm than good if viewed from a spiritual standpoint; it has polluted many families and caused social disintegration in many homes. So many parents have no time for their children again. They outfitted their homes with various electronic gadgets so that their children could feed on them.

I was forced to spend the night with a family sometime ago and happened to be with them. When I was there, I observed that nobody was conversing with one another. Everyone was engrossed in their phones. One of them, the youngest, who was only four years old, came to play with me. She attempted to play with me while asking if she belonged in their family.

I had to take her to her parents so they could hear her ask the same question again because I was unable to respond. The young girl appeared to have conveyed her message to the parents.

Another time, a man came to me with his daughter and her mother. Because the girl took a picture of herself while she was naked and unintentionally sent it to her father via social media video chat, the man was mad at both of them.

The girl's parents were devout, devoted Christians. The girl responded that she had always been alone and that no one was always available to speak with her; when I asked her why she had done such a thing, she said, "My mother is always in her shop, while my father is always traveling." " "Then I began making friends on social media, and that's how I met this guy who was always talking with me, and that's how our relationship began," she concluded. The parents realised their errors when they heard what the girl had to say.

It has been said that you can browse either God's or Satan's internet, depending on which one you prefer. Many people might believe this even though it lacks any biblical support. More negatives than positives can be said about the intrenet.

It makes people more inclined towards evil than good. In the Act of the Apostles, the believers prayed without technology or a public address system, and the place shook. How was that possible?

*"And when they heard it, they raised their voices together to God and said, "O sovereign Lord [having complete power and authority], it is You who made the heaven and the earth and the sea, and everything that is in them; it is You who, by the Holy Spirit, through the mouth of our father David, your servant, said, "Why did the nations [Gentiles] become arrogant and rage, and the peoples devise futile things [against the Lord]? The kings of the earth took their stand [to attack], and the rulers were assembled together against the Lord and against his anointed [the Christ, the Messiah]. For in this city there were gathered together against your holy servant Jess, whom you anointed, both Herod and Pontius Pilate, along with the Gentiles and the people of Israel, to do whatever your hand and your purpose predestined [before the creation of the world] to occur [and so, without knowing it, they served your own purpose]. And now Lord, observe their threats [take them into accounts] and grant that your bond-servants may declare your message [of salvation] with great confidence, while you extend your hand to heal, and signs and wonders [attesting miracles] take place through the name [and the authority and power] of your hold servant and son Jesus". And when they had prayed, the place where they were meeting together was shaken [a sign of God's presence], and they were all filled with the Holy Spirit and began to speak the word of God with boldness and courage. Acts 4:24–31 AMP*

It was the power of God that shook the place where the believers gathered to pray. However, in this day and age, it is technology and public address systems that always shake the place where we gather. There was something those men had that we in this generation have lost. It is spiritual stamina. The people of old were able to achieve so much because of the spiritual stamina they had.

The truth is that technology—TV, radio, the internet, and social media—are all poisonous if left uncontrolled without applying some level of discipline. During Daniel's time, the poison was the king's food, which was spiritual poison to his faith. How did I know that the food Daniel rejected was poison?

*"The king replied to the Chaldeans, "my command is firm and unchangeable; if you do not reveal to me the [content of the] dream along with its interpretations, you shall be cut into pieces and your houses shall be made a heap of rubbish. But if you tell [me] the content of the dream along with its interpretations, you shall receive from me gifts, rewards, and great honor. So tell me the dream and its interpretations. They answered again, "Let the king tell the dream to his servants, and we will explain its interpretation [to you]." If you will not reveal to me the [content of the] dreams, there is but one sentence for you; for you have [already] prepared lying and corrupt words [and you have agreed together] to speak [them] before me [hoping] to delay your execution until the situation is changed. Therefore, tell me the rest first, and then I will know with confidence that you can give me its interpretations. The Chaldeans answered the king and said, "There is not a man on earth who can tell the king this matter, for no king, Lord, or ruler has ever asked such a thing of any magician, enchanter, or Chaldean." Furthermore, what the king demands is indeed an unusual and difficult thing: "No one except the gods can reveal it to the king, and their dwelling is not with mortal flesh." Daniel 2:5-7, 9-11 AMP*

The royal court included the Chaldeans. They consumed the king's food and wine, but they were unable to obtain the disclosure of the secrets the king required. You cannot consume delectable poison and expect to comprehend the principles governing spiritual matters. Spiritual things are for those who can reach some level of discipline in dealing with the gates to their soul and spirit. You can't do anything the way you like and expect to get positive, exceptional results. The Bible says:

*"Deep calleth unto deep at the noise of thy waterspouts; all thy waves and thy billows are gone over me." Psalms 42:7 KJV.*

"Deep calls unto deep" means the deep things of God need the deepness of men before they can manifest into reality. You cannot eat what everyone else is eating and expect to be different from them. You need to go deeper to get the deep things of God.

If Daniel and his three friends had not dared to be different and go deeper, the whole people who ate the king's food and drank his wine would have died at the king's command. The magicians and Chaldeans could not see and understand the king's dream. Why? It was because of the delicious poison they had eaten. That delicious poison would have killed them if not for the intervention of Daniel and his friends.

They became aware that they had been consuming delicious poison when the death penalty was hanging around their necks. However, that discovery came too late to affect their outcome. Only Daniel and his friends had the power to alter events.

As Christians, may we not discover our mistakes when it is already too late. Amen. You may ask, "Why didn't they pray? I want to believe they prayed. But it is not all prayer; we pray that God answers. Some answers to some prayers come because of certain prices we have paid or are currently paying. While some answers to prayers are dependent on how far we have gone with God in obedience and love,

The Bible says:

*"Call unto me, and I will answer thee, and I will shew thee great and mighty things, which thou knowst not." Jeremiah 33:3 KJV.*

Yes, God said it; when we call to Him, He will answer; but if your calling to God is only when you are in trouble, prepare for more pain. God made this promise to a man. I mean a prophet of God who has a deep relationship with God. Jeremiah had a great relationship with God. God himself testified about him, saying.

*"Before I formed thee in the belly, I knew thee; and before thou camest forth forth out of the womb, I sanctified thee, and I ordained thee a prophet unto the nations. Jeremiah 1:5 KJV*

Do you truly understand God? Do you believe in God? It is one thing for us to assert that we know God, but quite another for him to acknowledge our mutual familiarity. Although many people assert that they know God, God does not know them. Where did I learn that?

*"And while they went to buy, the bridegroom came, and they that were ready went in with him to the marriage, and the door was shut. Afterward came also the other virgins, saying, "Lord, Lord, open to us. But he answered and said, "Verily, I say unto you, I know you not." Matthew 25:10–12 KJV.*

This is the story of ten virgins. Five of them were wise, and five were foolish. The foolish ones did not come to the meeting with extra oil. The wise ones were well prepared; they came to the meeting with extra oil, should the Lord delay coming to the meeting. The foolish ones ran out of oil and went outside to buy; by the time they returned, the Lord had come and the door was shut against them. Don't forget that they were still virgins. The way of God is different from our own. Sometimes, the answers to our prayers depend on our relationship with God. See what David said in the Psalms.

*"And call upon me in the day of trouble, and I will deliver thee, and thou shalt glorify me." Psalms 50:15 KJV*

As believers, we quote this verse most of the time when we pray, but we don't pay attention to the verse before that one. Before God will answer certain prayers, we need to have acted on verse fourteen, then God will act on verse fifteen, and we follow up in verse sixteen. Let's read from verse 14:

*14. Offer unto God thanksgiving; and pay thy vows unto the most high. 15. And call upon me in the day of trouble. I will deliver thee, and thou shalt glorify me. 16. But unto the wicked God he says, "What hast thou to do to declare my statutes, or that thou shouldst take my covenant in thy mouth? Psalms 50:14–16 KJV*

Another version says:

*14. Make thankfulness your sacrifice to God and keep the vows you made to the Most High. "Then call on me when you are in trouble, and I will rescue you, and you will give me glory." 16. But God says to the wicked: "Why bother reciting my decrees and pretending to obey my covenant? Psalms 50:14–16 NLT*

The other version of the Bible has given us a better understanding of those scriptures. For God to act and deliver us from our trouble at times, the conditions are in verse fourteen. We need to honour God, constantly give thanks, and live our lives as sacrifices to him. These are the qualifications to enter the realm when God acts as he promised in verse fourteen.

Check out what Daniel and his friends did when they were given the chance to live a life of pleasure and enjoyment. They denied themselves such pleasures. Have you denied yourself, as Jesus said?

*"And he was saying to them all, "If anyone wishes to follow me [as my disciple], he must deny himself [set aside selfish interest] and take up his cross daily [expressing a willingness to endure whatever may come] and follow me, believing in me, conforming to my example in living, and, if need be, suffering or perhaps dying because of faith in me." Luke 9:23 AMP*

This was what Daniel and his friends did in Babylon. It was a great opportunity and privilege to eat the king's food. But Daniel said no to it. Others who were with Daniel and his friends saw the opportunity to eat the king's food as promotion, while Daniel and his friends saw it differently.

It is only those who really know God who can escape the pollution that follows each generation. In our generation, pollution and defilement are not just in food and drink but also in technology, the internet, etc., which the devil has hijacked.

You are the only person who has the ability to choose to be right in the face of enormous injustice. Someone said, "You choose whom to browse in the world of computers because both good and bad are there. Both God and Satan are there.

I want to think that some of the young men who went through the training with Daniel and his three friends must have questioned why they wouldn't eat the food the king provided. They were unbothered by Daniel and his friends. They clung to the truth they had.

See what the Bible says in Psalm 50:16.

*"But God says to the wicked, "Why bother reciting my covenant?" Psalms 50:16NLT.*

This is what many people do when they are in trouble. It is only the trouble that makes them remember God. When the trouble is over, they return to their old ways. God is not bound to answer the prayers of such a person because he has no relationship with God.

What is the king's food you are feeding on? What we feed on now is not just food. Jesus said:

*"But Jesus replied, "It is written and forever remains written; man shall not live by bread alone, but by every word that comes out of the mouth of God." Matthew 4:41 AMP*

Jesus desires that we live by the word of God in the same way that we live by food. Our concern should not be only food without an interest in the word of God. Satan has turned the message upside down by feeding people damaging information. The chief of staff in the royal court in Babylon, who fed others with the king's food, was also the one who fed Daniel and his friends with vegetables.

In today's world, it will be difficult to live without technology, the internet, mobile phones, etc. It is left for you to choose how you want to use them. You don't need to allow the corruption and pollution these devices spread to come into your life.

Demons have possessed many people through television, the internet, video clips, mobile phones, etc. I have heard of some people who went for deliverance prayer, and the demons in them said that they possessed their victims through television, mobile phones, and video clips.

**The unknown doors in human beings.**

There are four doors in the human body through which demons can possess someone. These doors are the eyes, ears, mouth, and sexual organs. These are the doors demonic spirits depend on to possess people.

The first three doors are the ones that open the way to the fourth. When Satan came to the Garden of Eden, he could not do anything against Adam and Eve. He had to devise a strategy to build an information link "that can feed the ear, then the eyes, and eventually the mouth. He knew if he could go through these doors, he would get the woman's mind and heart.

*"Now the serpent was more crafty [subtle, skilled in deceit] than any living creature of the field that the Lord God had made. And the serpent [Satan] said to the woman. Can it really be that God has said, you shall not eat from any three of the garden?" Genesis 3:1 AMP*

This verse of the scripture tells us of the qualifications of the devil and how Satan was able to open the communication systems that linked the woman with him.

*And the woman said to the serpent, "We may eat fruit from the trees of the garden, except the fruit from the tree that is in the middle of the garden." God said, "You shall not eat from it nor touch it; otherwise, you will die." Genesis 3:2–3 AMP*

When the devil opened communication with the woman, she accepted and began to chat with Satan in verses 2 and 3.

*But the serpent said to the woman, "You certainly will not die! For God knows that on the day you eat from it, your eyes will be opened [that is, you will have greater awareness], and you will be like God, knowing the difference between good and evil. Genesis 3:4-5 AMP*

In verses four and five, Satan switched from just communication to information technology. The information Satan gave Eve opened her eyes to the need to eat the fruit.

*"And when the woman saw that the tree was good for food and that it was delightful to look at and a tree to be desired in order to make one wise and insightful, she took some of its fruit and ate it, and she also gave some to her husband with her, and he ate." Genesis 3:6 AMP*

Then in verse six, the woman used the information she got from verses four and five to feed her soul and spirit. The next thing was that she went for the fruit. Mind you! That tree has been in the garden for a long time. She did not see the need to eat from the tree until Satan came and opened her eyes to see that the tree was beautiful and a tree to be desired to make one wise.

Satan is still using the same information systems he used to destroy Adam and Eve in this generation.

## The Hidden Gold in You

The hidden gold in humans doesn't come out when they are in a pleasurable environment. This was the mistake of the king of Babylon. God also tried it, but it did not work. How did I know?

We follow this sequence in scripture:

*"The first Adam received life; the last Adam is a life-giving spirit. Physical life comes first, then spiritual—a firm base shaped from the earth, a final completion coming from out of heaven. ""The first man was made out of earth, and people since then have been earthy; the second man was made out of heaven, and people now can be heavenly." I Corinthians 15:45–48 MSG*

Adam started his ministry in the garden, the place of enjoyment and pleasure, and he failed. The last Adam [Jesus Christ] started his ministry in the wilderness, and he succeeded. The hidden gold in man can only come out in an environment of discipline, pain, and sweat.

This was the mistake of the king of Babylon, although he meant well for those he chose to serve in the royal court. He did not know that good food and wine could not make someone wise. The king's plan was to have people who would be part of his government and could provide him with any information he required.

*"The king told Ashpenaz, head of the palace staff, to get some Israelites from the royal family and nobility—young men who were healthy and hand-some, intelligent and well-educated, good prospects for leadership positions in the government, perfect specimens! And indoctrinate them in the Babylonian language and the love of magic and fortune telling". Daniel 1:3–4 MSG*

From verses three to four of that scripture, the plan of the king of Babylon was to get people who would serve him and be part of his government. The main reason he recruited young men was to get streams of information and hidden secrets from them. The fact that the king wanted the best from the men he recruited made him instruct the chief of staff to feed them with his own food and drink.

The majority of the gifted and talented people in the church occasionally have pretty poor character and attitude, which is something else I want us to see in Daniel 1:4. I welcome criticism! Have you ever noticed that the most talented people tend to live lives filled with unresolved issues? If Satan doesn't fill them with pride, they are typically haughty, flirtatious, and unyielding. This is the work of Satan.

The young men selected to work with the king were full of pride, but only four of them could understand what lay ahead of them.

*"The king then ordered that they be served from the same menu as the royal table—the best food and the finest wine. After three years of training, they would be given positions in the king's court". Daniel 1:5 MSG*

The king, who wanted the best, made a mistake by putting these young men into such a pleasurable life. He had no idea that pleasure made men weak, not strong. Christians who live unruly lives are to blame for the lukewarmness we observe in the church today.

When the church was under persecution, it grew stronger and better. The more believers were persecuted, the better they were. But Satan devised a means of weakening the church through pleasure.

*"And others had trial of cruel mocking and scourging, yea, moreover of bonds and imprisonment. They were stoned they were sawn asunder, were tempted, were slain with the sword; they wandered about in sheepskins and goatskins; being destitute, afflicted, tormented, [of whom the world was not worthy] they wandered in deserts, and in mountains, and in dens and caves of the earth". Hebrews 11:36–38 KJV*

The characters and faith of those early believers are revealed in that verse. This does not imply that God desires suffering for his children. Far from it, I say. God desires for his children to possess the world's wealth. However, sadly, only a small percentage of God's children who have inherited wealth have allowed it to possess them.

Daniel learned that if he consumed the king's food, the gold within him would not manifest. To reveal the hidden gold in him, he required a stressful situation and condition.

*"Indeed, I have refined you, but not as silver; I have tested and chosen you in the furnace of affliction." Isaiah 48:10 AMP*

This was the secret to the success of Daniel and his friends in Babylon. They forbidden themselves to take pleasure in the king's pleasure. By doing this, they were able to develop themselves beyond the king's expectations.

## The Disciplined Lifestyle

According to the Cambridge Dictionary, discipline is "the training that increases people's willingness to obey or capacity for self-control, frequently in the form of rules and consequences for breaking them" or "the behaviour produced by this training, the capacity for self-control or that of others, even in challenging circumstances." According to the Merriam-Webster dictionary, discipline is the process of obtaining control by enforcing obedience or order—the prescribed or ordered behaviour or pattern. Last but not least, as instruction that improves or moulds the moral or intellectual faculties.

These are the dictionaries' definitions of discipline. It is only discipline that will make someone not eat delicious poison. Because of the way the world is now, everything is going digital, and on the internet, discipline is the only way to live a spiritually sound life.

*"At the end of the time set by the king to bring all the young men in [before him], the commander of the officials presented them to Nebuchadnezzar. The king spoke with them, and among them all not one was found like Daniel, Hanniah, Mishael, and Azariah; so they were [selected and] assigned to stand before the king and enter his personal service". Daniel 1:8–19 AMP*

At the expiration of the period set by the king for the training of the young men, only four of them who did not eat the king's food really passed the king's test. The king took four of them into his personal service. The king must have thought that the four young men fed very well on the food and wine he provided.

He did not know that they achieved the feat through self-discipline. It is difficult to achieve anything spiritually significant without a considerable level of self-control. It is not possible to advise anybody not to use technology and social media now. But anyone who wants to serve God well should use those things with self-discipline and restraint. It is foolishness for one to allow anything to control his life apart from God. One of the men in the Bible I respect so much is Lot. He was a man of great discipline and self-control.

*The two angels arrived at Sodom in the evening. Lot was sitting at the city gate. He saw them and got up to welcome them, bowing before them and saying, "Please, my friends, come to my house and stay the night. Wash up. You can rise early and be on your way refreshed". They said, "No, we will sleep in the street." But he insisted and would not take "no" for an answer, and they relented and went home with him. Lot fixed a hot meal for them, and they ate. Before they went to bed, men from all over the city of Sodom, young and old, descended on the house from all sides and boxed them in. They yelled to Lot, "Where are the men who are staying with you for the night? ""Bring them out so that we can have our sport with them!' Lot went out, barring the door behind him, and said, "Brothers, please don't be vile! ""Look, I have two daughters, virgins; let me bring them out; you can take your pleasure with them, but don't touch these men—they are my guess." They said, "Get lost! ""You drop in from nowhere, and now you are going to tell us how to run our lives. ""We will treat you worse than they will!' and they charged past Lot to break down the door. But the two men reached out and pulled Lot inside the house, locking the door. Then they struck blind the men who were trying to break down the door, both leaders and followers, leaving them groping in the dark. The two men said to Lot, "Do you have any other family here? Sons, daughters—anybody in the city? Get them out here and now!"We are going to destroy this place. "The outcries of the victims here to God are deafening; we have been sent to blast this place into oblivion." Lot went out and warned the finances of his daughters, "Evacuate this place; God is about to destroy this city"! But his daughters' would be husbands treated it as a joke. At the break of day, the angels pushed Lot to get going, saying, "Hurry. ""Get your wife and two daughters out of here before it is too late and you are caught in the punishment of the city." Genesis 19:1–15 MSG*

Lot managed to survive in Sodom without turning gay because

he possessed a high degree of self-control and discipline. The same explanation explained why he was able to raise his two daughters, who remained virgins until Sodom was destroyed. He exercised self-control and constraint to avoid joining the city's residents in disobeying God.

*"God said, "If I find fifty decent people in the city of Sodom, I will spare the place just for them." Abraham came back, saying, "Do I, a mere mortal made from a handful of dirt, dare open my mouth again to my master?" "What if the fifty fell short by five?" "Would you destroy the city because of those missing five?" He said, "I won't destroy it if there are forty-five." Abraham spoke up again, "What if you only find forty?" "Neither will I destroy it for forty." He said, "master, don't be irritated with me, but what if I find thirty?" He pushed on, "I know I am trying your patience, master, but how about twenty?" "I won't destroy it for twenty." He would not quit. "Don't get angry, master; this is the last time. ""What if you come up with ten?" For the sake of only ten, I won't destroy the city. When God finished talking with Abraham, he left. "And Abraham went home." Genesis 18:26–33 MSG*

Ten good men would have prevented the destruction of Sodom and Gomorrah. To be able to live in a setting where the smell of homosexuality reached God's nostrils, Lot must have had a strong sense of high morality and great discipline.

Because people around you are eating delicious poison, you don't need to as well. You must learn to be disciplined and controlled in everything you do. More importantly, you must prioritise God in all that you do.

**Types of Discipline**

There are different types of discipline. But the three I want to discuss here are: divinely imposed discipline, externally imposed discipline, and self-imposed discipline.

1. Divinely Imposed Discipline

This is the type of discipline God imposes on individuals, especially his children, in order to train or correct them. There is divine discipline for the righteous.

*"The Lord gave another message to Jeremiah. He said, "Go down to the potter's shop, and I will speak to you there," so I did as he told me and found the potter working at his wheel. But the jar he was making did not turn out as he had hoped, so he crushed it into a lamp of clay again and started over. Then the Lord gave me this message. "O Israel, can I not do to you as this potter has done to his clay?" "As the clay is in the potter's hand, so are you in my hand." Jeremiah 18:1-6 NLT*

a. Divine Discipline for Punishment:

This happens when someone receives divine discipline for doing something wrong or committing sin.

b. Divine Discipline for Righteousness:

*"God blesses those who are persecuted for doing right, for the kingdom of heaven is theirs." Matthew 5:10 (NLT)*

*"You are blessed when your commitment to God provokes persecution. ""The persecution drives you even deeper into God's kingdom." Matthew 5:10 (MSG)*

Divine discipline for righteousness happens when believers suffer for doing the right thing. When that happens, the believers are expected to glorify and worship God for his suffering for righteousness' sake. The reason I called it "divine discipline" is that God allows it to happen. One of the versions of the scriptures above says, "This kind of discipline will drive you deeper into God's kingdom. An example is the story of Job.

1. Divine Discipline for Growth:

*"Every branch in me that does not bear fruit, He takes away; and every branch that continues to bear fruit, He [repeatedly] prunes, so that it will bear more fruit [even richer and finer fruit]." John 15:2*

I called this discipline, even though the branch is bearing fruit. The reason God still prunes it is to make sure it bears more fruit. Every believer must in one way or another experience this divine pruning; if not, there will be no growth in the person.

2. Externally Imposed Discipline

This type of discipline can be experienced by both believers and non-believers alike. It is imposed by superior authority on others to effect changes in their character or attitude. There are three types of externally imposed discipline:

a. Family imposed discipline:

This is the type of discipline a family gives to people to bring them up to become responsible members of society.

*"Train up a child in the way he should go, and when he is old, he will not depart from it." Proverbs 22:6 KJV*

*"Do not withhold discipline from the child; if you swat him with a reed-like rod [applied with godly wisdom], he will not die.""You shall swat him with the reed-like rod and rescue his life from the shoal [the nether world, the place of the dead]." Proverbs 23:12–14 AMP*

*"Don't be afraid to correct your young ones; a spanking won't kill them. A good spanking, in fact, might save them from something worse than death".* *Proverbs 23:12–14 MSG*

The Bible advises parents and family members to bring up children so they will be useful to themselves, their families, God, and society at large.

1. Master-servant, imposed discipline:

This is a training-based discipline. The master imposed discipline on the servant, and the servant subjected himself to the discipline of the master in order to get the training required of him.

It can also be called teacher-student discipline. The teacher imposed discipline on the student to modify the character of the student for the purpose of learning or acquiring certain knowledge.

*"Servants, obey in everything those who are your earthly masters, not only when their eyes are on you as pleasers of men, but in simplicity of purpose*

*[with all your heart] because of your reverence for the Lord and as a sincere expression of your devotion to him. Whatever may be your task, work at it heartily [from the soul] as [something done] for the Lord and not for menrs of men, but in simplicity of purpose [with all your heart] because of your reverence for the Lord and as a sincere expression of your devotion to him. Whatever may be your task, work at it heartily [from the soul] as [something done] for the Lord and not for men. Colossians 3:22–23 AMPC*

*"Servants [slaves], be obedient to those who are your physical masters, having respect for them and eager concern to please them, in simplicity of motive and with all your heart, as [service] to Christ [himself]." Ephesians 6:5 AMPC*

The master-servant relationship necessitates the servant's obedience to progress through the period of training.

1. Military-imposed discipline:

This is the discipline of the armed forces. The discipline is forceful and without any sense of pity. Here, people are trained and well-disciplined to become better officers for their nations.

1. Self-Imposed Discipline

*"Apply your heart to discipline and your ears to words of knowledge." Proverbs 23:12 AMP*

*"Give yourselves to disciplined instruction; open your ears to tested knowledge." Proverbs 23:12 MSG*

Self-imposed discipline is the best type of discipline. It is the type of discipline that is suitable for end-time believers. Both divinely imposed and externally imposed discipline have limitations in terms of achieving specific results.

It is only self-imposed discipline that has the ability to achieve what a person wants in life. This was the type of discipline Daniel and his friends applied in Babylon. Nobody forced Daniel and his friends not to eat the king's food and drink the wine. They decided not to eat it by themselves. Similarly, nobody is going to force you not to watch movies and films that can pollute and defile your soul and spirit. You are the only one who can stop yourself from imposing discipline on yourself.

Self-imposed discipline is the only way to build spiritual stamina. Let's hear from

Apostle Paul, who finished a successful race, said:

*"I have fought the good fight, I have finished the race, and I have remained faithful." 2 Timothy 4:7 NLT.*

*"I have fought the good [worthy, honorable, and noble] fight; I have finished the race; I have kept [firmly held] the faith." 2 Timothy 3:7 AMPC*

I want us to look at that scripture critically and pick out certain words Paul used to describe his experience with Timothy. These words are: fought, good, fight, finished, and race. The word "fought" is the past tense of "fight. This tells us that the war lasted for a long time. Paul told Timothy that ministry work was a fight that would last until glory was won. The word "good" tells us that there was a reason for the fight. He was not fighting for the wrong reasons.

Many believers are fighting for the wrong reasons today. The word "fight" reveals the strength and stamina Paul put into each battle he met. The word "finished" shows that there was a competition. Many people competed, but Paul was able to finish and become the winner. The word "race" shows that other people also ran for the prize he won. But not all who started were able to remain in the race till the end. Some people stepped aside.

*"For Demas has deserted me for love of this present world and has gone to Thessalonica; Crescens has gone to Galatia, Titus to Dalmatia." 2 Timothy 4:10 AMPC.*

Demas was in the race alongside Paul; he fought along with Paul. At some point, he dropped out of the race. Why did he drop out of the race? The answer is that he did not have enough spiritual stamina to continue the race. I want to believe that Demas ate delicious poison that made him derail from the faith. Another question is: who was Paul fighting against? The answer is simple. He was fighting himself. Does that shock you? I believe that Paul was constantly fighting himself and resisting the power of delicious poison. Paul said;

*"But [like a boxer], I buffet my body [handle it roughly, discipline it by hardship], and subdue it for fear that after proclaiming to others the gospel and things pertaining to it, I myself should become unfit [not stand the test, be unapproved, and be rejected as a counterfeit]." 1 Corinthians 9:27 AMPC*

From that scripture, you can know with whom Paul was fighting. Paul's greatest battle was against himself in 2 Timothy 4:7 vs. 7. In the same vein, we must fight against our appetite for delicious poison. Paul said he handled himself roughly. Anyone who wants to pet himself cannot escape the power of delicious poison.

*"I discipline my body like an athlete, training it to do what it should. Otherwise, I fear that after preaching to others, I myself might be disqualified." 1 Corinthians 9:27 NLT.*

How often have you taken time to train your body? The only way to train the body is through discipline. If you don't take time to train your body, your body will give you an unpleasant surprise one day.

Prayers:

1. I reject everything that looks good physically but spiritually has a death sentence on it in Jesus' name.
2. My father, my Lord, dips my body, soul, and spirit in the blood of Jesus and breaks off every delicious poison that weakens me spiritually in Jesus' name.
3. I received power to fight a good fight and to fight everything that fights against my soul in Jesus' name. Amen.
4. I receive the power to say no to delicious poison in Jesus' name.
5. I receive the power and the grace to apply discipline to my life in Jesus' name.

6. Oh, Lord, help me to discipline myself in order to bring glory to you in Jesus' name.

**6**

# The Jesus Yoke or the Satan Yoke?

Matt. 11:28–30.

The first thought that comes to mind when people hear the word "yoke" is one of evil. Not all yokes are bad; I want us to understand that. Both good and bad yokes exist. The main issue is who has authority over you or to whom you submit yourself. In order for us to better understand what I am saying, I want us to read from two different translations of the Bible.

*"Are you tired? Worn out? Religion is dead? Come to me. Get away with me, and you will recover your life. I will show you how to take a real rest. Walk with me and work with me—watch how I do it. Learn the unforced rhythms of grace. "I won't lay anything heavy or ill-fitting on you. ""Keep company with me, and you will learn to live freely and lightly." Matthew 11:28–30 MSG*

*"And come unto me, all ye that labour and are heavy laden, and I will give you rest. Take any yoke upon you and learn of me; for I am meek and lowly in heart, and you shall find rest for your souls. My yoke is easy, and my burden is light. Matthew 11:28–30 KJV*

We want to see the yoke that Jesus told us to take and why he wanted us to take it.

What is a yoke?

A yoke is a wooden crosspiece that is fastened around the necks of two animals and attached to the plough or cart that they are to pull, according to the dictionary.

Wikipedia puts it this way:

A yoke is a wooden beam that is typically used between two animals, such as oxen, to enable them to pull together on a load when working in pairs. Some yokes are fitted to individual animals as well. Different cultures and oxen require different yokes of various types.

The Yoke of Jesus

To be yoked to something is to be bound together. Such a union enables the two things to work together to accomplish a specific objective. The yoke of Jesus is different from a human yoke.

The burden of the human yoke is great and hard to bear. But everyone can easily bear the light burden of the yoke of Jesus. Jesus' teachings and way of life were evidence of his yoke. Christ yoked himself to the Father in heaven; that was why he succeeded.

He wants us to submit to him so that we can share in his success. We cannot please God unless we yoke ourselves to Jesus. Jesus' desire to please and serve the Father dates back to his early years.

*"And when he was twelve years old, they went up to Jerusalem after the custom of the feast. And when they had fulfilled the days, as they returned, the child Jesus tarried behind in Jerusalem, and Joseph and his mother knew nothing of it. But they, supposing him to have been in the company, went a day's journey, and they sought him among their kinsfolk and acquaintance. And when they did not find him, they turned back to Jerusalem, seeking him again. And it came to pass, after that three days they found him in the temple, sitting in the midst of the doctors, both hearing them, and asking them questions. And all who heard him were astonished at his understanding and answers. And when they saw him, they were amazed, and his mother said to him, "Son, why hast thou dealt with us? Behold, thy father and I have sought*

*you in sorrow. And he said unto them, "How is it that ye seek me? ""Wist ye not that I must be about my father's business? "And they understood not the saying which he spoke unto them." Luke 2:42–50 KJV*

Jesus realised at the age of twelve that in order to carry out the will of the father, he had to yoke himself to the father. Even when animals are yoked together, they cannot really work to achieve the needed result without the direction of the owners.

*"And he was withdrawn from them about a stone's cast, and kneeled down, and prayed, saying, "Father, if thou be willing, remove this cup from me; nevertheless, not my will but thine be done." Luke 22:41–42 KJV*

The passage from the Bible that we just read demonstrates that Jesus was joined by his heavenly father. What was the yoke of Christ like? It was his death and the cross. How was Jesus able to accomplish it? He yoked himself to the father and followed the father's instructions.

*"So Jesus explained himself at length. "I am telling you this straight. The son can't independently do a thing, only what he sees the father doing. What the father does, the son does. The father loves his son and includes him in everything he is doing. But you haven't seen the half of it yet, for in the same way that the father raises the dead and creates life, so does the son. The son gives life to anyone he chooses. Neither he nor the father shut anyone out. The father handed all authority to judge over to the son so that the son would be honored equally with the father. Anyone who dishonours the son, dishonours the father, for it was the father's decision to put the son in the place of honour". John 5:19–20 MSG*

*"This is because I have never spoken on my own authority, of my own accord, or as one who is self-appointed, but the father who sent me has himself given me orders [concerning] what to say and what to tell [Deut. 18:11, 19]. And I know that this commandment is [means] eternal life. So whatever I say, I am saying [exactly] what my father has told me to say and in accordance with his instructions". John 12:49–50 AMPC*

*"I have told you this ahead of time, before it happens, so that when it does*

*happen, the confirmation will deepen your belief in me. I will not be talking with you much more like this because the chief of the godless world is about to attack. But don't worry; he has nothing on me, no claim on me. But so the world might know how thoroughly I love the father. I am carrying out my father's instructions right down to the last details. "Get up; let's go. It's time to leave here" John 14:29–31 MSG*

*"For I have come down from heaven not to do my own will and purpose, but to do the will and purpose of him who sent me." John 6:38 A.M., P.C.*

The scriptures we read reveal that Jesus yoked himself to the father and followed the father's instructions to the end. I want us to go back to the main text of our discussion, which is  Matthew 11:29–30.

*"Take my yoke upon you and learn of me, for I am gentle [meek] and humble [lowly] in heart, and you will find rest [relief and ease, refreshment, recreation, and blessed quiet] for your souls [Jer. 6:16] "For my yoke is wholesome [useful, good—not harsh, hard, sharp, or pressing, but comfortable, gracious, and pleasant], and my burden is light and easy to bear." Matthew 11:29–30 AMPC.*

"Learn from me," Jesus said in the text above. The Bible's message translation reads, "Walk with me and work with me." If we don't take lessons from Jesus, there is no way that we can be successful Christians. If we don't walk and work with Jesus Christ, our Lord, our relationship with God will be worthless. We will be able to follow his instructions and directions if we do this.

*"If you keep my commandment [if you continue to obey my instructions], you will abide in my love and live on in it, just as I have obeyed my father's commandment and lived on in his love." John 15:10 AMPC*

If we want to please Jesus Christ, our Saviour, we must yoke ourselves to him. This is what the Apostle Paul meant by "dying daily."

*"I have been crucified with Christ [in him I have shared his crucifixion]; it is no longer I who live, but Christ [the Messiah] lives in me, and the life I now live in the body I live by faith in [by adherence to, reliance on, and complete*

*trust in] the son of God, who loved me and gave himself up for me." Galatians 2:20 AMPC*

Paul, the apostle, claimed that he could no longer please people or himself because he had accepted the yoke of Jesus. Paul was constantly focusing on how he could please his master. Let's make every effort to yoke ourselves to Jesus Christ. You should be aware that there is no middle ground when it comes to serving God if we refuse, as some have already done. Either you yoke yourself to Christ directly or you yoke yourself to someone else indirectly.

*"This is war, and there is no neutral ground.""If you are not on my side, you are the enemy; if you are not helping, you are making things worse." Matthew 12:30 MSG*

*"He who is not with me [definitely on my side] is against me, and he who does not [definitely] gather with me and for my side scatters. Matthew 12:30 (AMP.C.)*

By this point, you must have a better understanding. This is war, the Bible declares. That is to say, both God and Satan are interested in having you on their team. You are free to decide which side you want to support. If you haven't developed a strong enough spiritual foundation, you won't be able to stand by God's side. You must yoke yourself to Jesus Christ and be willing to die every day in order to accomplish this. You must also completely silence your flesh.

*"Now every athlete who goes into training constructs himself temperately and restricts himself in all things. They do it to win a wreath that will soon wither, but we do it to receive a crown of eternal blessedness that cannot wither. Therefore, I do not run uncertainly [without a definite aim]. "I do not box like one, beating the air and striking without an adversary. "But [like a boxer], I buffet my body [handle it roughly, discipline it by hardship], and subdue it for a year, so that after proclaiming to others the gospel and things pertaining to it, I myself should become unfit [not stand the test, be unapproved, and be rejected as a counterfeit]." 1 Corinthians 9:25–27 AMPC.*

Jesus desires our sincere service to him. We must yoke ourselves to Jesus Christ if we are to serve God honestly. His yoke, he claimed, is light and simple. How much lighter than Satan's yoke is the yoke of Jesus?

You must understand that accepting Jesus' yoke will ensure your eternal life in the heavenly kingdom. while Satan's yoke will result in eternal damnation in hell.

In other words, a yoke can be a form of influence. If you are a follower of Christ, the Holy Spirit will direct and inspire you to aid others in gaining access to God's kingdom. However, Satanic influence always results in humiliation and destruction. Those who live under Christ's yoke are known as [USED AND REWARDED].

used and rewarded.

When animals are yoked together for farming or other purposes, their owner must feed them afterward so that they will have enough energy to carry out the same tasks again. God rewards individuals after using them to accomplish certain objectives.

Satan has no provision for rewarding those he uses. Saul, who later became Paul, was under the influence or yoke of the devil. He persecuted the church until Jesus met him and set him free.

*"Meanwhile, Saul still drawing his breath hard form threatening and murderous desire against the disciples of the Lord, went to the high priest and requested of him letters to the synagogues at Damascus [authorizing him], so that if he found any man or woman belonging to the way [of] life as determined by faith in Jesus Christ], he might bring them bound [with chains] to Jerusalem. Now as he traveled on, he came near Damascus, and suddenly a light from heaven flashed around him, and he fell to the ground. Then he heard a voice saying to him, "Saul, Saul, why are you persecuting me?" [harassing, troubling, and molesting me] And he said, "Who are you, Lord? And he said, "I am Jesus, whom you are persecuting. It is dangerous, and it will turn out badly for you to keep kicking against the goal [to offer vain and perilous resistance]. Trembling and astonished, he asked, "Lord, what do you desire me to do? The Lord said unto him, "Arise and go into the city, and you*

*will be told what you must do. The man who were accompanying him were unable to speak [for terror], hearing him were unable to speak [for terror], hearing the voice but seeing no one". Acts 9:1–7 AMPC*

When Saul repented, he gave his whole life to serving Jesus Christ, and later he became Paul, an apostle of Jesus Christ. Before then, Saul was under the yoke of Satan, working tirelessly to fulfil the mission of Satan. When Paul was under the total influence of Jesus Christ, he also worked tirelessly to make sure that he pleased his master. At the end of his walk with Christ on earth, he was hopeful of getting some rewards from his master.

*"As for me, my life has already been poured out as an offering to God. The time of my death is near. I have fought the good fight, I have finished the race, and I have remained faithful. And now the prize awaits me—the crown of righteousness, which the Lord, the righteousness judge, will give me on the day of his return. ""And the prize is not just for me but for all who eagerly look forward to his appearing." 2 Timothy 4:6–8 NLT.*

That scripture shows that anyone who serves God wholeheartedly cannot go without some rewards. This scripture is enough to encourage believers to be more dedicated to God in their services, knowing that they will be rewarded at the end of their mission on earth. To achieve what he did, the apostle Paul had to endure a great deal of suffering for the sake of Christ.

*"There was a disciple in Damascus by the name of Ananias. The master spoke to him in a vision. "Ananias". Yes master". He answered. Get up and go over to Straight Avenue. Ask at the house of Judas for a man from Tarsus. His name is Saul. He is there praying. He has just had a dream in which is serious. Everybody is talking about this man and the terrible things he has been doing—his reign of terror against your people in Jerusalem! And now he has shown up here with papers from the Chief Priest that gave him license to do the same to us." But the master said, "Don't argue. Go!" "I have picked him as my personal representative to non-Jews, kings, and Jews. ""And now I am*

*about to show him what he is in for with the hard suffering that goes with this Job." Acts 9:10–16 MSG*

Jesus Christ delivered Saul of Tarsus from the yoke of Satan and put him under his own yoke. God is still doing the same thing he did for Saul. All we need to do is hold fast to the right doctrines in God's word and remain faithful to God. The apostle Paul yoked himself to Jesus to the point that he called himself a prisoner of Jesus Christ.

*"Therefore, I, a prisoner for serving the Lord, beg you to lead a life worthy of your calling, for you have been called by God." Ephesians 4:1 NLT*

Why did Paul call himself a prisoner of Jesus? First of all, as a prisoner, he was restricted from doing many things he would have loved to do. He could not eat quality food. In a nutshell, he had no access to the good things of life because of the gospel he was preaching. We should learn from the example of the apostle Paul. He had the opportunity to live a life of pleasure, but he rejected it in order to serve his master very well. We also need to become prisoners of Christ in order to develop the spiritual capacity that will help us finish the race. There is another man who was under the yoke of Satan but later became an evangelist for Christ.

*"They came to the other side of the sea to the region of the Gerasenes. And as soon as he got out the boat, there met him out of the tombs a man [under the power] of an unclean spirit. This man continually lived among the tombs, and none could subdue him anymore, even with a chain; for he had been bound often with shackles for the feet and handcuffs, but the handcuffs of [light] chains he wrenched apart, and the shackle he rubbed and ground together and broke in pieces, and no one had strength enough to restrain or tame him. Night and day among the tombs and on the mountains, he was always shrieking and screaming, beating and bruising himself, and cutting himself with stones. And when, from a distance, he saw Jesus, he ran and fell on his knees before him in homage. And crying out with a loud voice, he said, "What have you got to do with me, Jesus, son of the most high God? [What is there in common between us?] I solemnly implore you, by God, do not begin to torment me! For Jesus was*

*commanding, "Come out of the man, you unclean spirit! And he asked him, "What is your name? He replied, "my name is Legion, for we are many. And when he had stepped into the boat, the man who had been controlled by the unclean spirits kept begging him that he might be with him. But Jesus refused to permit him, but said to him, "Go home to your own [family, relatives, and friends] and bring word back to them of how much the Lord has done for you and how he has had sympathy for you and mercy on you. And he departed and began to publicly proclaim in Decapolis [the region of the ten cities] how much Jesus had done for him, and all the people were astonished and marveled [Matt. 4:25], Mark 5:1–9, 18–20 AMPC.*

Before being freed by Jesus Christ, this man was completely under the devil's control. He was plagued by a multitude of demons who tormented him every day. He lived close to mountains and tombs. Without Christ, this man would have perished in the terrible condition that Satan had placed him in.

But Jesus showed him mercy and set him free. Having expressed his gratitude to God, he started sharing the good news of Jesus Christ with those in the city. We will have the fortitude and spiritual fortitude required to finish the race under the yoke of Jesus. Without providing them with rewards, God cannot call people to serve him. God respects his kids and would never disgrace them.

*"But the firm foundation [laid by] God stands, sure and unshaken, bearing this seal [inscription]. "The Lord knows those who are His, and let everyone who names himself by the name of the Lord give up all iniquity and stand aloof from it." 2 Timothy 2:19 AMPC.*

May God give us the ability to yoke ourselves to Jesus Christ in order to be useful ambassadors of Christ.

The Yoke of Satan

Jesus said, "Come unto me, all ye that labour and are heavy-laden. Labour and heavy loads imply Satan's yoke. Jesus Christ forbade believers from accepting Satan's yoke.

*"That made the world as a wilderness, and destroyed the cities thereof; that opened not the house of his prisoners". Isaiah 14:17 KJV*

According to the Bible, Satan doesn't let his prisoners' homes be opened. Satan employed a number of strategies to draw people to himself. But sin is always the main tool he employs to yoke both men and women to himself. Since the fall of man in the Garden of Eden, Satan has put mankind under his yoke and influence. Sometimes the yoke of Satan looks like freedom for those who are under it. But, in reality, it is both a yoke and a burden.

According to Jesus' call, coming to Jesus means laying aside the weight of sin and turning to Christ. Many people are burdened by many things in life. Before Christ set me free, I was enslaved to sex, pornography, and theft.

What are the things to which you are bound? You are unable to free yourself from Satan's yoke on your own. Give your heart to God, and he will deliver you, just as he did for me. Jesus has the power to bring you out of the prison of Satan. Remember how Satan tormented the man he held among the tombs? The man tried to free himself but could not. You will not also let Jesus help you out.

*"Night and day among the tombs and on the mountains, he was always shrieking and screaming, beating and bruising himself, and cutting himself with stones." Mark 5:15 AMC*

The man was genuinely tortured. He was unable to get himself out of trouble on his own. He was rescued from the devil's torment by Jesus. The same Jesus is prepared to relieve you of all your current suffering. He will assist you if you repent and turn to him.

The Yoke of Sin

Sin is the greatest yoke anyone can put on themselves. Sin can destroy anyone, whether they are rich or poor, black or white. Sin is indifferent to personality or race. Sin is the force that operates within people and compels them to do things against their will.

*"Knowing this, that our old man is crucified with him, that the body of sin might be destroyed, that henceforth we should not serve sin". Romans 6:6 KJV*

The Bible advises us not to serve sin. This means that sin has the ability to dominate someone and reduce him to a slave. Someone who allows sin to rule their life is just waiting for trouble. We must abide by the teachings of Jesus in order to prevent sin from taking over our lives.

*"When a defiling evil spirit is expelled from someone, it drifts along through the desert looking for an oasis, some unsuspecting soul it can bedevil. When it doesn't find anyone, it says, "I will go back to my old haunt." On return it finds the person spotlessly clean, but vacant. It then runs out and winds up seven other spirits more evil than itself, and they all move in, whooping it up. That person ends up far worse off than if he had never gotten cleaned up in the first place". That is what this generation is like. You may think you have cleaned out the junk from your lives and gotten ready for God. "But you were not hospitable to my kingdom message, and now all the devils are moving back in." Matthew 12:43–45 MSG*

It is preferable for someone who has been freed from the yoke of Satan to be filled with the word of God and the Holy Spirit. After being delivered, the devil will return if one is empty. We should not create a vacuum for the devil to fill in our lives. When we are set free, we should not allow the power of this world to entice us again into sin. Let's see how Satan enticed Eve into sinning against God.

*"The serpent was clever, more clever than any wild animal God had made. He spoke to the woman, saying, " Do I understand that God told you not to eat from any tree in the Garden?" The woman said to the serpent, "Not at all. We can eat from the trees in the middle of the garden, but God said, "Don't eat from it; don't even touch it, or you will die." The serpent told the woman, "You won't die. God knows that the moment you eat from that tree, you will see what is readily going on. ""You will be just like God, knowing everything, ranging all the way from good to evil. ""When the woman saw that the tree looked like good food and realized what she would get out of it, she would know everything! ""She took and ate the fruit and then gave some to her husband, and he ate." Genesis 3:1–6 MSG*

Eve was led to commit a sin against God by Satan, but he kept this information from her. Instead, Satan offered Eve his package as a chance to enjoy life. Satan is still using this method to make people fall into sin. The sin of Adam and Eve spread and became a universal problem.

*"For all have sinned and come short of the glory of God." Romans 3:23 KJV*

Most of the time, Satan does not compel people to submit to his yoke. He plays tricks by highlighting the advantages and benefits of people obeying him. When someone chooses the devil's option, he locks them up in his prison.

*"You are of your father, the devil, and it is your will to practice the lusts and gratify the desires, which are characteristics of your father. He was a murderer from the beginning and does not stand in the truth because there is no truth in him." "When he speaks falsehood, he speaks what is natural to him, for he is a liar [himself] and the father of lies and of all that is false." John 8:44 AMPC.*

In that verse, Christ refers to the devil as "your father," implying that the people were under his rule and influence. People always experience shame and destruction under the devil's influence. However, we will find peace and rest when we yoke ourselves to Christ. We should do everything in our power to avoid letting sin rule us.

*"Sin shall not have dominion over you; for you are not under the law but under grace." Romans 6:14 KJV*

*"That means you must not give sin a vote in the way you conduct your lives. Don't give it the time of day. Don't even run little errands that are connected with that old way of life. Throw yourselves wholeheartedly and fully—remember, you have been raised from the dead!—into God's way of doing things. Sin cannot tell you how to live. After all, you are not living under that old tyranny any longer. You are living in the freedom of God's love in the way you conduct your lives. Don't give it the time of day. Don't even run little errands that are connected with that old way of life. Throw yourselves wholeheartedly and fully—remember, you have been raised from the dead!—into*

*God's way of doing things. Sin cannot tell you how to live. After all, you are not living under that old tyranny any longer. You are living in the freedom of God. Romans 6:12–14 MSG*

The burden of sin is awful. Sin has the power to keep a person in perpetual darkness without light. Jesus Christ has the power to free you from any addiction to sin. Reconcile yourself to him and confess your sin.

The Yoke of Religion

I want us to take our Bible reading from the Message Bible to get a better understanding of this topic.

*"Are you tired? Worn out? Burned out on religion? Come to me and say, "Get away with me, and you will recover your life." Matthew 11:28 MSG*

"Religion" is yet another oppressive burden that the devil has placed on people. Satan has used religion to oppress people and still does. Religion is powerless to prevent people from sinning against God. In a similar vein, religion is powerless to deliver humanity from the devil.

The word of God through Jesus Christ is the only thing that can keep a person from transgressing against God. When people turn to God in sincere repentance, Jesus' blood will atone for their transgressions. Today, there are so many people who are still living in sin and are obediently attached to various religions. This implies that they will not be able to escape God's judgement.

used and dumped

Satan's business is to use people and then dump them. He doesn't have any plans to reward those who work for him.

*"Then Satan entered Judas Iscariot, who was one of the twelve disciples, and he went to the leading priests and captains of the temple guard to discuss the best way to betray Jesus to them. They were delighted, and they promised to give him money. So he agreed and began looking for an opportunity to betray Jesus so they could arrest him when the crowds were not around". Luke 22:1–3 NLT.*

By opening himself up, Judas allowed Satan to enter him. Why did

Satan sneak up on him? Judas was taken by the devil because he was a tool for him. Judas was actually dumped and used by the devil.

Being used and dumped by someone can be a painful experience. One day, I saw a lady who was crying bitterly. When I questioned her friend about the issue, she revealed that the woman had been taken advantage of and dumped by a man.

From their father, the devil, many people have learned without even being aware of it. A great number of people serve Satan as his agents. Some people carry on doing something even though they are aware that it is wrong. Others willfully commit sin and then beg God for forgiveness.

*"Lord, Lord, have we not prophesied in your name, driven out demons in your name, and done many miracles in your name? And then I will declare to them publicly, "I never knew you; depart from me [you are banished from my presence], you who act wickedly [disregarding my commands]." Matthew 7:21–23 AMP*

One of the Bible passages that terrifies me the most is this one. The reason for this is

that many churchgoers mistakenly believe that God is using them when, in fact, Satan is doing the same.

Consider a scenario in which Jesus tells a pastor or general overseer: "I do not know you; depart from me, you worker of iniquity. What follows is the query: Whom did the pastor serve? He served the devil, after all. He never had a job with God. In the church, he spent his days doing the devil's bidding. What a loss! There won't be any justification for such dissatisfaction if someone can truly take the yoke of Christ upon himself.

Prayers

1. Oh, God, if you will reject, reject, or punish anything? Let it not be me, in Jesus' name.
2. Father, search me and remove all the things that do not bring you glory in my life, in Jesus' name.
3. Father, do not allow the devil to use me in Jesus' name.

4. Oh, Lord, my helper, never allow the voice of the flesh to be louder than the voice of the spirit in my life.
5. I reject and refuse every yoke of Satan in my life.

# CHAPTER 7

7

# *Seven Steps to Building Spiritual Stamina*

Building spiritual strength can be accomplished in a number of ways. I'll outline seven of them for you here. For every Christian who wants to run the race and come out on top, spiritual endurance is crucial. In my opinion, you can develop the spiritual stamina you need to run and prevail in the race by following these seven steps.

The first step is obedience.

Obedience:

One of the crucial factors that can facilitate our relationship with God is obedience. Obedience has the power to create or take away life. Adam and Eve serve as classic illustrations of how disobeying instructions can make life miserable. I want us to read about the life of a man in the Bible.

*"And Enoch walked with God; and it was not for God that he took him." Genesis 5:24 KJV*

*"And [in reverent fear and obedience], Enoch walked with God; and he was not found among men, because God took him [away to be home with him]." Genesis 5:24 AMP*

Readings from the Bible reveal that Enoch walked in fear with

135

God and obeyed his commands. The power of obedience transformed Enoch's body, soul, and spirit because he obeyed God during his time on earth. He needed to be brought to heaven by God while still alive. In the same vein, disobedience has the power to bring shame, destruction, and death to the people.

*"So then, as through one trespass [Adam's sin] there resulted condemnation for all men, even so, through one act of righteousness, there resulted justification of life for all men.""For just as through one man's disobedience [his failure to hear, his carelessness] the many were made sinners, so through the obedience of one man the many will be made righteous and acceptable to God and brought into right standing with Him." Romans 5:18–19 AMP*

Both obedience and disobedience have benefits and drawbacks. They both possess the ability to bless and curse. People can achieve greatness and great success by being obedient. Satan is aware that God operates within the bounds of laws and order and that disobedience brings people down and turns them from glory to shame.

He went to Eve and inquired about any rules that God had given them to follow. Eve responded in the affirmative, and we must abide by the prohibition against eating the fruit of the tree of the knowledge of good and evil. Eve was then led to disobey God by Satan.

*"Now the serpent was more crafty [subtle, skilled in deceit] than any living creature of the field that the Lord God had made. And the serpent [Satan] said to the woman, "Can it really be that God has said, you shall not eat from any of the trees of the garden?" Genesis 3:1 AMP*

*"The serpent was clever, more clever than any wild animal God had made. He spoke to the woman. "Do I understand that God told you not to eat from any tree in the Garden?" Genesis 3:1 MSG*

The way the devil put his question to the woman shows that Satan was looking for a reason to make her disobey God.

*"So the creation of the heavens and the earth and everything in them was completed. On the seventh day, God had finished his work of creation, so he rested from all his work. And God blessed the seventh day and declared it*

*holy, because it was the day when he rested from all his work of creation".*
*Genesis 2:1–3 NLT.*

God rested after completing the work of creation. Apart from man, everything God created followed His commands. Man's disobedience to God's command prevented God from taking true rest. As a result of its disobedience to God's word, man, or humanity, is unable to find rest.

*"So then, there is still awaiting a full and complete Sabbath-rest reserved for the [true] people of God. For he who has once entered [God's] rest also has ceased from the weariness and pain of human labor, just as God rested from those labors peculiarly his own [Gen. 2:2]. Let us therefore be zealous and exert ourselves and strive diligently to enter that rest [of God, to know and experience it for ourselves]that no one may fall or perish by the same kind of unbelief and disobedience [into which those in the wilderness fell].  Hebrews 4:9–11 AMPC*

"A child who does not allow his mother to sleep cannot sleep himself," according to an African proverb.

Since man has not obeyed the commandments of God, he too has not found rest and peace for himself.

*"I have seen the travail, which God hath given to the sons of men to exercise in it".  Ecclesiastes 3:10 KJV*

*"I have seen the painful labor and exertion and miserable business which God has given to the sons of men with which to exercise and busy themselves."*
*Ecclesiastes 3:10 AMPC*

*"And I gave my heart to seek and search out wisdom concerning all things that are done under heaven.  This sore travail hath God given to the sons of men to be exercised therewith". Ecclesiastes 1:13 KJV*

King Solomon wrote these scriptures from two perspectives. The first point of view stemmed from his time as King of Israel and his research. The divine inspiration he received was the second point of view. Remember that Adam did not begin his life in the Garden of Eden in pain. Mankind's tribulation was brought about by disobedience to God's word. Let us review the punishment God meted out to Adam and Eve after they sinned.

*"Unto the woman, he said, I will greatly multiply thy sorrow and thy conception in sorrow thou shalt bring forth children; and thy desire shall be to thy husband, and he shall rule over thee. And unto Adam he said, because thou hast hearkened unto the voice of thy wife, and hast eaten of the tree, of which I commanded thee, saying, thou shalt not eat of it; cursed is the ground for thy sake; in sorrow shalt thou eat of it all the days of thy life; thorns also and thistles shall it bring forth to thee; and thou shall eat the herb of the field; in the swat of thy face shalt thou eat bread, till thou return unto the ground; for our of it was thou taken; for thou art dust, and unto dust shalt thou return".Genesis 3:16–19 KJV*

When Adam and Eve disobeyed God, he commanded all of creation to rebel against Adam. God cursed Eve by lowering her spiritual status and making childbirth painful for her. The curses of Adam and Eve were passed down to all of humanity. Mankind is still busy carrying out Adam and Eve's curses. In his wisdom, King Solomon put it this way:

*"To everything there is a season, and a time to every purpose under the heaven. A time to be born, and a time to die; a time to plant, and a time to pluck up that which is planted; a time to kill, and a time to heal; a time to break down, and a time to build up; "A time to weep, and a time to laugh; a time to mourn, and a time to dance," a time to cast away stones, and a time to gather stones together; a time to embrace, and a time to refrain from embracing; a time to get and a time to lose; a time to keep and a time to cast away; a time to rend, and a time to sew; a time to keep silent, and a time to speak; a time to love, and a time to hate; a time for war, and a time for peace. What profit hath he that worketh in that wherein he laboureth? "I have seen the travail which God hath given to the sons of men to be exercised in it." Ecclesiastes 3:1–10 KJV*

The problem with mankind is that it is disobedient to the word of God. To avoid the travail King Solomon talked about and enter into the rest and peace of God, we must obey God's word.

*"Then, there is still awaiting a full and complete Sabbath-rest reserved for the [true] people of God; for he who has once entered [God's] rest also his ceased from [the weariness and pain] of human labour, just as God rested form those labours peculiarly his own [Gen. 22]. Let us therefore be zealous and exert ourselves and strive diligently to enter that rest [of God, to know and experience it for ourselves], that no one may fall or perish by the same kind of unbelief and disobedience [not which those in the wilderness fell]".* Hebrews 4:9–11 AMPC

The only way to obtain Sabbath rest is to obey God's word as revealed through Jesus. As a result, obedience is an important step in developing spiritual stamina for end-time believers. Apart from spiritual matters, we must obey whenever we are subject to a higher authority.

For example, if a student refuses to listen to his teachers' instructions, he will fail his exams. Similarly, anyone in any career or vocation who refuses to obey his superior officers' orders cannot excel. In God's kingdom, obedience is like breathing. This means that without obedience, no one can survive in God's kingdom. Obedience was what allowed Enoch to have a fruitful relationship with God. It is impossible to maintain fellowship with God without obedience.

Endurance:

Endurance is a tremendous virtue. It is a virtue that anyone who wishes to excel in any aspect of life must possess. It is uncommon to find someone who has attained greatness without practicing endurance. Endurance, like obedience, is a skill that must be honed. There are no laws or methods that can force someone to develop endurance. It is practiced in difficult, harsh, and horrifying situations and conditions. God has the attribute of endurance.

*"Do you see what this means—all these pioneers who blazed the way; all these veterans cheering us on? It means we had better get on with it. Strip down, start running, and never quit! No extra spiritual fat, no parasitic sins. Keep your eyes on Jesus, who both began and finished this race we are in. Study how he did it. Because he never lost sight of where he was headed—that*

*exhilarating finish in and with God—he could put up with anything along the way: a cross, shame, whatever. And now he is there, in the place of honor, right alongside God. When you find yourselves flagging in your faith, go over that story again, item by item, that long litany of hostility he plowed through. That will short adventive into your souls!' Hebrews 12:1-3 MSG*

*"Therefore, since we are surrounded by such a huge crowd of witnesses to the life of faith, let us strip off every weight that shows us down, especially the sin that so easily trips us up. And let us run with endurance the race God has set before us. We do this by keeping our eyes on Jesus, the champion who initiates and perfects our faith. Because of the joy awaiting him, he endured the cross, disregarding its shame. Now he is seated in the place of honor beside God's throne. "Think of all the hostility he endured from sinful people; then you won't become weary and give up." Hebrews 12:1–3 NLT*

Endurance was one of the qualities that enabled the "heroes of faith" to succeed in their missions. Even our Lord and Saviour, Jesus Christ, practiced endurance in order to achieve the greater glory that lay ahead of him. We also need to work on our endurance. As I previously stated, there is no level of anointing or principle that will provide you with endurance. It is something you must put into practice in your daily life. People who were not noble by birth or status became great because they practiced endurance.

I once saw a heavyweight boxing champion's interview. He was asked how he came from behind to win the championship. "I have to take all of my opponent's punches," he replied. When his punches landed on my body, they were heavier than 150 kg, so I had to endure and stay focused until he was exhausted." After that, I attacked him back. "I won and became champion by enduring his punches. Life, like the story of the boxing champion, will throw heavy punches at you, as will Satan; what you need to do is endure to overcome them.

*"But watch thou in all things, endure afflictions, do the work of an evangelist, make full proof of thy ministry". 2 Timothy 4:5 KJV*

In that scripture, Paul the apostle told Timothy to endure afflictions.

He did not tell him to fast and pray to avoid affliction. Endurance is what every true Christian must practice. In another place, Paul encouraged Timothy to learn how to practice endurance as part of his calling.

*"Thou therefore endure hardness as a good soldier of Jesus Christ. No man that warreth entangled himself with the affairs of this life; that he may please him who hath chosen him to be a soldier. And if a man also strive for masteries yet he is not crowned, except he strive lawfully". 2 Timothy 2:3-5 KJV*

*"Endure suffering along with me as a good soldier of Christ Jesus. Soldiers don't get tied up in the affairs of civilian life, for then they cannot please the officer who enlisted them.""An athlete cannot win the prize unless they follow the rules." 2 Timothy 2:3-5 NLT.*

Paul compared the Christian's walk and work to military service, in which each soldier is rigorously trained to meet the demands of his job. The apostle Paul compares God's work to two types of professions: soldier and athlete. Because of the nature of their professions, these individuals understand what endurance entails. Soldiering entails difficult and painful training; to enlist, one must endure hardship.

In other words, in order to become a soldier, one must endure the difficult and painful aspects of his training. Similarly, an athlete An athlete works out his body in all areas that will help him succeed. As a result, an athlete may subject himself to painful training, forego pleasure, and do other things in order to win a race.

These few words of prayer and encouragement may help you practice endurance.

*Lord, I am weary, and I don't know when this "race" will end in my life. I feel like I have been running forever, trying to outrun this trial. Help me stop trying to outrun my pain, but rather, run with endurance the race you have set before me. I know that because of you, I am ultimately a victor over the trials in my life. I know that nothing in this world can separate me from your steadfast love. Please give me a measure of your love today; give me the strength to endure this trial. Thank you for your love for me that never ends.*

*And thank you for the crown of joy that awaits me in your kingdom. In Jesus' name, Amen.*

**Pure Motive:**

When it comes to God, motives are extremely important. Nobody can serve God with the wrong motive and succeed spiritually in God's business. God does not require people who serve him for the wrong reasons. Many people attend church for a variety of reasons. Some are motivated by a desire to serve God honestly, while others are motivated by a desire to make money through the church. There are also those who seek to obstruct God's work. Let us examine the Bible to see how God dealt with those who came to church with malicious intent.

*"Afterward they traveled from town to town across the entire island until finally they reach Paphos, where they met a Jewish sorcerer, a false prophet named Bar-Jesus. He had attached himself to the governor, Sergius Paulus, who was an intelligent man. The governor invited Barnabas and Paul to visit him, for he wanted to hear the word of God. But Elymes, the sorcerer [as his name means in Greek], interfered and urged the governor to pay no attention to what Barnabas and Paul said. He was trying to keep the governor from believing. Saul, also known as Paul, was filled with the Holy Spirit, and he looked the sorcerer in the eye. Then he said, "You son of the devil, full of every sort of deceit and fraud, and enemy of all that is good!" "Will you never stop perverting the true ways of the Lord?" "Watch now, for the Lord has laid his hand of punishment upon you, and you will be struck blind." "You will not see the sunlight for some time." Instantly, mist and darkness came over the man's eyes, and he began groping around, begging for someone to take his hand and lead him. When the governor saw what had happened, he became a believer, for he was astonished at the teaching about the Lord". Acts 13:6–12 NLT.*

This man had the wrong motivation when it came to God's things. Even though he was Jewish, his motivation was to obstruct God's work. He attempted to keep the governor from knowing and accepting the truth of God's word. His goal was to obstruct God's work. He attempted to keep the governor from knowing and accepting the truth of God's word. The apostle Paul had to silence him through the power of the Holy Spirit. Simon of Samaria was another church member with a bad motive.

*"Then Peter and John laid their hands on these believers, and they received the Holy Spirit. When Simon saw that the Holy Spirit was given when the apostles laid their hands on people, he offered them money to buy this power. "Let me have this power, too," he exclaimed, "so that when I lay my hands on people, they will receive the Holy Spirit!" But Peter replied, "May your money be destroyed with you for thinking Dolly's gift can be bought! You can have no part in this, for your heart is not right with God. Repent of your wickedness and pray to the Lord. Perhaps he will forgive your evil thoughts, for I can see that you are full of bitter jealousy and are held captive by sin". "Pray to the Lord for me," Simon exclaimed, "that these terrible things you have said won't happen to me!" Acts 8:17–24 NLT*

This man's motivations were heinous. He believed that the church of God was a place where anyone could conduct any business they desired. Second, this man desired to purchase the power of the Holy Spirit in order to use it in his own business. The apostle Peter knew the thoughts of this man and advised him to repent to avoid the judgement of God. The good thing about him was that he accepted repentance.

This man represents many people in the church. They are attending church for the purpose of gaining something. Their motivation is to profit from whatever they do in the church. Some were preaching the gospel during the apostle Paul's ministry not because they loved Christ or wanted to convert souls to God, but because they wanted to compete with Paul as an apostle of Christ. Their motivations for preaching the gospel were deplorable. Some preach out of jealousy and rivalry, and it is true. Others, on the other hand, preach about Christ with good intentions.

*"They preached because they loved me, for they knew I had been appointed to defend the good news. Those others do not have pure motives, as they preached about Christ. They preach with selfish ambition, not sincerely,*

*intending to make my chains more painful for me. but that doesn't matter.* *""Whether their motives are false or genuine, the message about Christ is being preached either way, so I rejoice. ""And I will continue to rejoice." Philippians 1:15–18 NLT.*

This is the true situation in the Church of God today. Some are serving God with the right motives, while others are doing so with the wrong motives. The truth is that any man who serves God with wrong motives cannot experience growth in his spirit. Today's churches are full of pastors, prophets, bishops, and apostles with the wrong motives. Most of them have the motive of making money and becoming famous.

This explains why they developed alternate abilities that could assist them in achieving their goals. It is the wrong motives that render our pastors, prophets, apostles, and bishops spiritually powerless. The majority of them are ordinary church administrators who lack God's power and knowledge.

Anyone, including non-believers, can help with the work they are currently doing in church. Our religious leaders must repent. They must abandon their arrogance and return to God. There are also people in the church who claim to serve God, but the Bible reveals that they are serving their stomach, and their stomach is their God.

*"Let all who are spiritually mature agree on these things. If you disagree on some point, I believe God will make it plain to you. But we must hold on to the progress we have already made. Dear brothers and sisters, model your lives after mine and learn from those who follow our example. For I have told you often before, and I say it again with tears in my eyes, that there are many whose conduct shows they are really enemies of the cross of Christ. They are headed for destruction. "Their God is their appetite; they brag about shameful things; and they think only about this life here on earth." Philippians 3:15–19 NLT*

These types of worshippers and leaders abound in today's church of God. The primary reason they attend church is to receive material blessings. Some pastors enjoy bragging about their wealth and other material possessions. They have no understanding of the things of

God's kingdom. Husbands and wives were another group of church-goers who had ulterior motives.

*"But there was a certain man named Ananias, who with his wife, Saphira, sold some property. He brought part of the money to the apostles, claiming it was the full amount. With his wife's consent, he kept the rest. Then Peter said, ""Ananias, why have you let Satan fill your heart? You lied to the Holy Spirit, and you kept some of the money back for yourself. The property was yours to sell or not sell, as you wished. And after selling it, the money was also yours to give away. How could you do a thing like this?"You were not lying to us, but to God!" As soon as Ananias heard these words, he fell to the floor and died. Everyone who heard about it was terrified. Then some young men got up, wrapped him in a sheet, and took him out and buried him. About three hours later, his wife came in, not knowing what had happened. Peter asked her, "Was this the price you and your husband received for the land?""Yes," she replied, "that was the price." And Peter said, "How could the two of you even think of conspiring to test the spirit of the Lord like this?""The young men who buried your husband are just outside the door, and they will carry you out too." Instantly, she fell to the floor and died. When the young man came in and saw that she was dead, they carried her out and buried her beside her husband. "Great fear gripped the entire church and everyone else who heard what had happened." Acts 5:1–11 NLT*

Ananias and Sapphira, husband and wife, died in the church because they served God with the wrong motives. They didn't fully believe in what they were doing. They reasoned that if they ran into problems, they could rely on the money they kept at home. They were not devout believers. God was furious with them, and he had to kill them to serve as a warning to others.

*"There are several reasons that make people serve God with wrong motives. Some of these reasons are: self-glorification, hunger for power and fame, wealth and money, jealousy, and pride. We should know that whatever we do in the church, the day of judgment will prove the motive behind our work.*

*Because of God's grace to me, I have laid the foundation like an expert builder. Now others are building on it. But whoever is building on this foundation must be very careful. For no one can lay any foundation other than the one we already have—Jesus Christ. Anyone who builds on that foundation may use a variety of materials—gold, silver, jewels, wood, hay, or straw. But on the judgment day, fire will reveal what kind of work each builder has done. "The fire will show if a person's work has any value." I Corinthians 3:10–11 NLT*

The value of each believer's service to the God-centred church will be revealed on the day of God's judgment. The name of God is being misused by many in the church for selfish ends. God doesn't serve them; they make God serve them. They only have earthly success as their motivation for joining the church. While still engaging in sin, some prophesy and perform miracles in the name of Jesus.

*"Not everyone who calls out to me, Lord! Lord, I will enter the kingdom of heaven. Only those who actually do the will of my father in heaven will enter. On judgment day, many will say to me, "Lord! Lord! We prophesied in your name, cast out demons in your name, and performed many miracles in your name. But I will reply, "I never knew you. "Get away from me, you who break God's laws." Matthew 7:21–23 NLT.*

It is extremely dangerous to attend church with ulterior motives. Wrong motives usually lead to destruction and shame.

When Elisha served Elijah, he did it with the right motive. But when Gehazi served Elisha, he did it with a bad motive. And as a result of his wrong motives, he loses his health as well as the health of future generations?

**Love what God loves and hate what God hates.**

The appropriate values and priorities are the focus of this discussion. The majority of churchgoers don't always put God's things first. Their moral compass is not in line with what God wants. We have to establish a set of principles that will respect God in whatever we do. Mary and Martha's narrative will teach us how to set priorities in our lives.

*"As Jesus and the disciples continued on their way to Jerusalem, they came to a certain village, where a woman named Martha welcomed him into her home. Her sister, Mary, sat at the Lord's feet, listening to what he taught. But Martha was distracted by the big dinner she was preparing. She came to Jesus and said, "Lord, doesn't it seem unfair to you that my sister just sits here while I do all the work?" Tell her to come and help me". But the Lord said unto her, "my dear Martha, you are worried and upset over all these details! There is only one thing worth being concerned about. ""Mary has discovered it, and it will not be taken away from her." Luke 10:38–42 NLT*

When Jesus and his disciples came to visit Mary and Martha, Martha focused on preparing food for them, while Mary sat down to listen to what Jesus was saying. Humanly speaking, Martha was acting appropriately at the time. Martha wanted to take care of their visitors by feeding them. Was that a bad thing? The answer is no. But, according to Jesus, it was not a valid thing to do at the time.

Jesus Christ did not value food as much as the word of God. He understood the importance of food for the body, but the spiritual food on Christ's mind was the word of God, which to Him was more valuable. Mary chose to receive spiritual food from the master, whereas Martha chose to provide physical food to her visitors.

Jesus told Martha that she had chosen the best, which is God's word. Jesus Christ taught Mary things of eternal value, whereas Martha was more interested in things of temporal value. Martha was encouraged by Jesus to prioritize her life by paying attention to what he was teaching. Martha had to put aside the temporal in order to hear the words of the King of Kings.

*"For the word of a king is authority and power, and who can say to him, "What are you doing?""Whoever observes the [king's] command will experience no harm, and a wise man's mind will know both when and what to do." Ecclesiastes 8:4-5 AMPC*

Mary received the word of God, which helped her build the spiritual stamina she needed to follow Jesus to the end. As a result, Mary was among the women who went to Jesus' tomb after he rose from the dead.

*"So the women left the tomb quickly, with fear and great joy, and ran to [tell the good news to] the disciples. And as they went, suddenly, Jesus met them, saying, "Rejoice!" And they went to him and took hold of his feet [in homage] and worshipped him [as the Messiah]. Matthew 28:8–9 AMP*

What we need to value most in the church is God's word. Serving God with honesty should be our priority in life. With his word, God created everything. In the church, His word should be supreme. With the power of his word, Jesus fed five thousand men in the wilderness.

*When evening came, the disciples came to him and said, "This is an isolated place, and the hour is already late; send the crowds away so that they may go away; you give them something to eat!" They replied, "We have nothing here except five loaves and two fish." Then he ordered the crowds to sit down on the grass, and he took the five loaves and the two fish and, looking up toward heaven, he blessed and broke the loaves and gave them to the disciples, and the disciples gave them to the people, and they all ate and were satisfied. They picked up twelve full baskets of the leftover broken pieces. an isolated place, and the hour is already late; send the crowds away so that they may go away; you give them something to eat!" They replied, "We have nothing here except five loaves and two fish." Then he ordered the crowds to sit down on the grass, and he took the five loaves and the two fish and, looking up toward heaven, he blessed and broke the loaves and gave them to the disciples, and the disciples gave them to the people, and they all ate and were satisfied. They picked up twelve full baskets of the leftover broken pieces. Matthew 14:15–17, 19–20 AMP*

Everything is possible through the word of God. Food was not as important to Christ as people receiving the word of God. When they had received the word, he did not allow them to go hungry, as the disciples anticipated. Jesus fed the people spiritually and physically with his word. The word of God is capable of doing anything—solving every problem and providing for every need.

*"The voice of the Lord is upon the waters: The God of glory thundereth; The Lord is upon many waters. The voice of the Lord is powerful; the voice of the Lord is full of majesty. The voice of the Lord breaks the cedars of Lebanon. He maketh them also to skip like a calf; Lebanon and Simon like a young unicorn. The voice of the Lord divided the flames of fire. The voice of the Lord shakes the wilderness; the Lord shakes the wilderness of Kadesh. "The voice of the Lord maketh the hinds to calve, and they have discovered the forests; and in his temple doth everyone speak of his glory." Psalms 29:3–9 KJV*

By the word of God, Mary gained spiritual ascendancy, whereas Martha did not. Many Christians are weak and unserious nowadays because there is no word of God in them. Martha later learned that the right priority and value were in the word of God.

Jesus taught Martha that the word of God had the highest priority and value at all times. Martha was not angry; she simply followed Jesus Christ's advice. Unlike John the Baptist, who was offended by Jesus' statement and had his life cut short by Herod.

*"John's disciples brought word to him [in prison] of all these things. John called two of his disciples and sent them to the Lord, asking, "Are you the expected one [the Messiah], or should we look for someone else?" At that very hour, Jesus healed many people of sicknesses, infirmities, and evil spirits, and he gave [the gracious gift of] sight to many who were blind. So he replied to them, "Go and tell John about everything you have seen and heard: the blind receive sight, the lame walk, the lepers are cleansed, the deaf hear, and the dead are raised up, and the poor have the good news [the gospel] preached to them. Blessed [joyful spiritually favoured] is he who does not take offense at me".Luke 7:18–23 AMP*

John the Baptist erred when he assumed that Jesus would operate according to standards and values that are human. Instead, Jesus followed a set of divine principles. John was most likely not receiving messages from the Holy Spirit at that point. That may have been the cause of his uncertainty about Jesus' status as the Messiah. John the Baptist's ministry was cut short by the devil through Herodias.

*"She, being coached by her mother [Herodias], said, "Give me here on a platter the head of John the Baptist." The king was distressed, but because of his oaths and because of his dinner guests, he ordered that it be given to her. He sent for John and had him beheaded in prison. His head was brought on a platter and given to the girl, and she brought it to her mother [Herodias]. And John's disciples came and took away the body and buried it. Then they went and told Jesusther [Herodias], "Give me here on a platter the head of John the Baptist." The king was distressed, but because of his oaths and because of his dinner guests, he ordered that it be given to her. He sent for John and had him beheaded in prison. His head was brought on a platter and given to the girl, and she brought it to her mother [Herodias]. And John's disciples came and took away the body and buried it. Then they went and told Jesus. Matthew 14:8–12 AMP.*

Herodias desired to assassinate John the Baptist, but she was unable to do so. She saw an opportunity to do so in King Herod's "open check" to her daughter. God desires for us to have spiritual understanding in order to grow in his word. The things of God were preferred by early believers over the temporal things of this life.

*"Some were jeered at, and their backs were cut open with swords." Others were chained in prisons. Some died by stoning, some were sewn in half, and others were killed with the sword. Some went about wearing the skins of sheep and goats, being destitute, oppressed, and mistreated. "They were too good for this world, wandering over deserts and mountains, hiding in caves and holes in the ground." Hebrews 11:36–38 NLT*

The Bible here talks about the heroes of old. Their thought lines were quite different from what we see in the church now. They did not see anything good enough in this world that would make them value the system of this world more than the things of God. These people only loved what God loved and hated what God hated. As Christians, we need to change our value system to align with that of God.

We must continue to serve God until the very end if we want to develop spiritual endurance. Without such a shift in priorities, we will keep pretending to serve God while actually serving only ourselves. When Jesus noticed that Peter's value had shifted from being the fisher of men to being a regular fisherman, he questioned him.

*"After these things Jesus shewed himself again to the disciples at the sea of Tiberias; and on this wise shewed he himself. There were together Simon Peter and Thomas, called Didymus, Nathanael of Cana in Galilee, the sons of Zebedee, and two other of his disciples. Simon Pete said unto them, I go a fishing. They say to him, "We also go with you. They went forth and entered a ship immediately, and that night they caught nothing. But when the morning was now come, Jesus stood on the shore, but the disciples knew not that it was Jesus. Then Jesus said unto them, "Children, have ye any meat? They answered him, "No," and he said unto them, "Cast the net on the right side of the ship, and ye shall find. They cast, therefore, and now they were not able to draw it for the multitude of fishes. Therefore, that disciple whom Jesus loved said to Peter, "It is the Lord. Now when Simon Peter heard that it was the Lord, he girt his fisher's coast unto him [for he was naked], and did cast himself into the sea. And the other disciples came in a little ship; [for they were not far from the land but as it were two hundred cubit], dragging the net with fishes. As soon as they got to the land, they saw a fire of coals there, and there were fish laid out and bread. Jesus saith unto them, bring of the fish which ye have now caught. Simon Peter went up and drew the net to a land full of great fishes—an hundred and fifty-three in all—and for all that there were so many, the net was not broken. Jesus said unto them, "Come and dine. And none of the disciples asked him, "Who art thou? knowing that it was the Lord. Jesus then cometh and taketh bread, and giveth them, and fish likewise. This is now the third time Jesus shewed himself to his disciples, after that he was risen from the dead. So when they had dined, Jesus said to Simon Peter, the son of Jonas, "Lovest thou me more than these? He said unto him, "Yea, Lord; thou knowest that I love thee. He said unto him, "Feed my lambs. He said to him again the second time, "Simon, son of Jonas, lovest thou me? He said to him, "Yea, Lord, you know that I love you. He said unto him, "Feed my*

*sheep. He said unto him the third time, "Simon, son of Jonas, lovest thou me? Peter was grieved because he said to him for the third time, "Lovest thou me? And he said unto him, "Lord, thou knowst all things; thou knowst that I love thee. Jesus said to him, "Feed my sheep." John 21:1-17KJV.*

This scripture shows that Peter abandoned the work Jesus gave him to do for his former job. As the leader of the group, Peter needed to organise them into an evangelical team instead of returning to fishing again. This implies that his regard for spiritual matters has shifted. Jesus inquired of Peter whether he loved him [Jesus] more than earthly things.

Peter said yes. Christ asked the question again, and Peter said yes. When Christ asked the question a third time, Peter was upset because he loved his master, and the master knew Peter loved him. But Peter did not realise that claiming to love his master without serving him was not enough.

Jesus was telling Peter that if he loved him, he would make his value equal to his. What was Christ's worth? to have the soul won into the kingdom of God. Many people have gone fishing in various areas of life, but they continue to pretend to serve God. They have replaced godly values with worldly values. Jesus observed a shift in value in the seven churches of Asia.

*"Unto the angel of the church of Ephesus write; these things saith he that holdeth the seven stars in his right hand, who walketh in the midst of the seven golden candlesticks, nevertheless I have somewhat against thee, because thou hast left thy first love". Revelation 2:1,4 KJV*

The church of Ephesus shifted its value from the love of God to something else. Similarly, you need to check your life as a Christian if you have not shifted your love for God towards worldly things.

*"And to the angel of the church in Pergamos write; these things saith he which hath the sharp sword with two edges; But I have a few things against thee, because thou hast there them that hold the doctrine of Balaam, who taught Balak to cast a stumbling block before the children of Israel, to eat things sacrificed unto idols, and to commit fornication". Revelation 2:12, 14 KJV*

Previously, this church taught sound doctrine. They altered their doctrine at some point, most likely to attract more members. This represents a change in the value of God's things.

.

*"And unto the angel of the church in Thyatira write; these things saith the son of God, who hath his eyes like unto flames of fire, and his feet are like fine brass, I know thy works, and charity, and service, and faith, and patience, and thy works; and the last to be more the first. Notwithstanding, I have a few things against thee, because thou sufferest that woman Jezebel, who called herself a prophetess, "to teach and to seduce my servants to commit fornication and to eat things sacrificed to idols." Revelation 2:18–20 KJV*

This church also shifted their value system to something else. They permitted certain evil practices in the Church of God. Out of the seven churches in Asia, only two churches held to the values they started with.

*"And to the angel of the church in Philadelphia write; these things saith he that his holy, he that is true, he that hath the key of David, he that opoeneth, and no man shutteth and no man openeth, I know thy works, behold I have set before thee an open door and no man can shut it; for thou has a little strength, and hast kept my word and not denied my name. Behold, I will make them of the synagogue of Satan, which say they are Jews, and are not, but do lie, Behold, I will make them to come and worship before thy feet and to know that I loved thee. Because thou has kept the word of my patience, I also will keep thee from the hour of temptation, which shall come upon all the world, to try them that dwell upon the earth.*

*Revelation 3:7–10 KJV*

*And to the angel of the church in Smyrna, write, "These things say the first and the last, which was dead and is alive; I know your works, your tribulations, and your poverty [but you are rich], and I know the blasphemy of them who say they are Jesus but are not, but are the synagogue of Satan. Fear none of these things which thou shall suffer: behold, the devil shall cast some of you into prison, that ye may be tried: and ye shall have tribulation ten days: be thou faithful unto dead, and I will give thee a crown of life".* Revelation 2:8-10KJV.

We need to constantly hold on to divine values that will enable us to run the race to the end.

Step Out in Faith:

When faced with certain problems, some Christians resort to complaining rather than stepping out in faith to confront the issues. We must be aware that there are forces working against the manifestation of glory in individuals. Faith in God's word is one of the weapons used to launch such forces.

When we rely on God to solve our problems, we demonstrate our faith in him. This is accomplished through regular prayer and Bible study. Certain doubts begin to fade from our hearts as we study and pray, and we gain confidence in God's word.

*"But without faith it is impossible to please him for he that cometh to God must believe that he is, and rewarder of them that diligently seek him".* Hebrews 11:6 KJV

God exists outside of time and space as we know them. God is revealed to us through his word and creation. To build faith, we must study God's word and believe what it says about our lives, health, marriages, businesses, and so on. The Message Bible puts it this way:

*"By an act of faith, Enoch skipped death completely. They looked all over and could not find him because God had taken him." We know on the basis of reliable testimony that before he was taken, he pleased God." It is impossible to please God apart from faith. And why? "Because anyone who wants to approach God must believe both that he exists and that he cares enough to respond to those who seek him." Hebrew 11:5–6 MSG*

Enoch was able to avoid death by exercising faith. Nothing is impossible with God when faith is applied. To obey God, one must have faith in him. And it takes obedience to demonstrate your faith in God. The Bible encourages Christians to fight for their faith.

*"Beloved, when I gave all diligence to write unto you of the common*

*salvation, it was needful for me to write unto you and exhort you that you should earnestly contend for the faith that was once delivered unto the saints. "For there are certain men who crept in unawares, who were before of old ordained to this condemnation, ungodly men, turning the grace of our God into lasciviousness, and denying the only Lord God and our Lord Jesus Christ." Jude 1:3–4 KJV*

*"My dear friends, I was doing my best to write to you about the salvation we share in common when I felt the need to write at once to encourage you to fight on for the faith that once and for all God has given to his people. For some godless people have slipped in unnoticed among us, persons who distort the message about the grace of our God in order to excise their immoral ways, and Lord. Long ago, the scriptures predicted the condemnation they have received".Jude 1:3–4 NLT*

How can we be satisfied with our faith? by staying true to God's word. We must not allow false teachers and prophets to lead us astray into devilish doctrine. We should also be wary of anything that seeks to undermine our faith and hope in the power of redemption found in Jesus' blood.

To step out in faith also means to cleave to God so that we cannot do without Him in every area of our lives. Faith is tested in the face of difficulty and problems. Someone who has not been tested through trials, problems, and difficulty cannot really claim to have faith.

Problems and difficulties arise to test whether or not a person believes in God. The benefit of developing spiritual stamina is that it allows you to deal with the problems and difficulties that come your way as a Christian. A weak man can become a very strong man through the exercise of faith, and a poor man can become rich. There are no limits to what faith can accomplish.

*"And what shall I say further? For time would fail me to tell of Gideon, Barak, Samson, Jepthah, of David and Samuel and the prophets, [Judges 4:1-5, 6:1-8, 35, 11:1-12, 13: 1-16; 1 Samuel 1-30; 2 Samuel 1-24,1 Kings 1-2; Acts3:24] who by the help of faith subdued kingdoms, administered justice, obtained*

*promised blessings, closed the mouth of lions,[Daniel 6] Extinguished the power of ragging fire, escaped the devouring of the sword, out of frailty and weakness won strength and became stalwart, even mighty and resistless in battle, routing aliens hosts [Daniel 3][some] women received again their dead by a resurrection. Others were tortured to death with clubs, refusing to accept release [offered on the terms of denying their faith] so that they might be resurrected to a better life. [1 Kings 17: 17-24; 2 Kings 4: 25- 37] others had to suffer the trial of mocking and scourging and even chains and imprisonments. They were stoned to death; they were lined with tempting offers [to renounce their faith]; they were sawn asunder; they were slaughtered by the sword; [while they were alive] they had to go about wrapped in the skins of sheep and goats, utterly destitute, oppressed, and cruelly treated—men of whom the world was not worthy—roaming over the desolate places and the mountains and [living] in caves and caverns and holes of the earth. "And all of these, though they won divine approval by [means of] their faith, did not receive the fulfillment of what was promised, because God had us in mind and had something better and greater in view for us, so that they [these heroes and heroines of faith] should not come to perfection apart from us [before we could join them]." Hebrews 11:32–40 AMPC*

Faith is essential in spiritual matters. Joshua showed confidence in the face of day-and-night challenges by telling the sun and moon to stand, which they dutifully obeyed. When we walk in faith with God, we can follow Him fearlessly. Peter experienced precisely this. The sight of someone strolling by the sea frightened them. However, Peter bravely walked on top of the water as soon as he heard the voice of Jesus Christ.

*"Then Jesus made the disciples get into the boat and go on ahead to the other side of the lake, while he sent the people away. After sending the people away, he went up a hill by himself to reach Ray. When evening came, Jesus was there alone, and by this time the boat was far out in the lake, tossed about by the waves because the wind was blowing against it. Between three and six*

*o'clock in the morning, Jesus came to the disciples, walking on the water. When they saw him walking on the water, they were terrified. "It is a ghost!' they said, screaming with fear. Jesus spoke to them at once. "Courage!' He said, "It is I; don't be afraid!' Then Peter spoke up to the Lord, "If it is really you, order me to come out on the water to you." "Come!' Jesus answered. So Peter got out of the boat and started walking across the water to Jesus. But when he noticed the strong wind, he was afraid and started to sink in the water. "Save me, Lord!' he cried. At once, Jesus reached out and grabbed hold of him and said, "What little faith you have!' "Why did you doubt?" They both got into the boat, and the wind died down. Then the disciples in the boat worshipped Jesus. "Truly, you are the son of God!' they exclaimed". Matthew 14:22–23 GNT.*

You, too, must take a leap of faith. Peter did it because he believed in Jesus Christ. All of the disciples, including Peter, were terrified at first. But when Peter realised it was Jesus, his fear dissipated, and he had the confidence to do what his master was doing. As Peter walked on the sea, he turned his attention away from Jesus and towards the wind, which caused him to sink. No matter what problems we face, we must continue to look to Jesus as the author and finisher of our faith. Looking elsewhere will only make our problems worse.

**Feed on the word of God.**

Nobody can grow up physically healthy if they do not consume the nutrients their bodies require. In the same way, no one can build spiritual stamina unless they feed on God's word. Jesus said that men should not live solely on bread but also on the words of God.

*"But he replied, It has been written, "Man shall not live and be upheld and sustained by bread alone, but by every word that comes from the mouth of God." [Deut 8:3] Matthew 4:4 AMPC*

The older generations of Christians knew this secret. They succeeded in gaining spiritual stamina, which helped them through the persecution. Always preserve God's word in our hearts.

*"I have not departed from his commands, but have treasured his words more than daily food." Job 33:12 NLT.*

*"I have not gone back from the commandment of his lips; I have esteemed and treasured the words of his mouth more than my necessary food." Job 23:12 AMPC*

The only food that the human spirit can consume and grow on is the written word of God. Your spirit man will grow thinner and shorter until it resembles a dwarf if the word of God is not fed to it. whereas your flesh will act like a complete fool in the spiritual realms. When you study the Bible, you are consuming God's word, which will make you a giant in the spirit. And Satan will find it challenging to convince you to abandon your faith.

*"Study to show thyself approved unto God, a workmen that needed not to be ashamed, but rightly dividing the word of truth". Timothy 2:15 KJV*

God will give you specific gifts from the kingdom of God when you are firmly established in his words and comprehend what the kingdom of God entails. Our body, soul, and spirit can all be changed by the power of the word of God. This is the rationale behind why we must constantly keep His words in our hearts.

*"Your word have I laid up in my heart, that I might not sin against you." Psalms 119:11 AMPC*

The ability to stop us from sinning against God comes from storing God's word in our hearts. Additionally, we must constantly reflect on God's word. And in order to meditate, we had to keep the words inside of us. When we use the words we have memorised to pray, act, or sing praises to God, we are doing meditation on those words.

*"I will meditate on your precepts and have respect for your ways [the paths of life marked out by your law]." [Psalm 104:34] Psalm 119:15.*

*"I will delight myself in your statutes; I will not forget your word". Psalm 119:16 AMPC*

*"The princes also sat and talked against me, but your servant meditated on your statutes." Psalm 119:23 AMPC*

*"Make me understand the way of your precepts; so shall I meditate on and talk of your wondrous works." [Ps. 145:5-6] Psalm 119:27.*

Daily Bible meditation is crucial to your spiritual growth. One cannot overstate the significance of recalling, remembering, and reciting the words of God. Our body, soul, and spirit will change as a result of proper daily meditation on God's word. We can continue to develop our spiritual strength in Christ in this way.

*"And I will walk at liberty and at ease, for I have sought and inquired for [and desperately required] your precepts". Psalm 119:45 AMPC*

*"I am yours; therefore, save me [as your own]; for I have sought [inquired of and for] your precepts and required them [as my urgent need]." [Ps. 42:1] Psalm 119:94 AMPC*

All we can do is strive to please God by following his instructions. We must become more like Jesus Christ than we currently are. We also need to talk about God's word all the time. The lessons found in God's word must be applied to every situation and facet of our existence.

*"Then shall I have an answer for those who taunt and reproach me, for I lean on, rely on, and trust in your word. ""And take not the word of truth utterly out of my mouth, for I hope in your ordinances." Psalm 119:42–43 AMPC*

*"I will speak of your testimonies also before kings, and I will not be put to shame." [Ps. 138:1; Matt. 10:18, 19; Acts 26:1; 2] Psalm 119:46 AMPC*

My faith has been bolstered by consistently hearing the word of God. Preaching the word of God to others is an additional facet of this. This hymn has the ability to fill your heart with the pleasure of the Lord. To become the person that Christ desires us to be, you must make time each day to read the Bible.

*"I have earnestly remembered your name, O Lord, in the night, and I have observed your law." Psalm 119:55 AMPC*

*"My eyes anticipate the night watches, and I am awake before the cry of the watchman, that I may meditate on your word." Psalm 119:148 AMPC*

Study your Bible on a daily basis. God will cause his spirit to guide you and lead you into the mystery of his words.

*"For whatever was written in earlier times was written for our instruction,*

*so that through endurance and the encouragement of the scriptures we might have hope and overflow with confidence in his promises." Romans 15:4 AMP*

This verse counsels us to study the Bible in order to gain the fortitude and inspiration we require from God's word. Another interpretation reads as follows:

*"Study this book of instruction continually. Meditate on it day and night so you will be sure to obey everything written in it. "Only then will you prosper and succeed in all you do." Joshua 1:8 NLT*

The greatest book ever written is the Holy Bible. Those who read and follow the instructions in the Bible are given life. The holy Bible contains God's thoughts and purposes for people. God instructed Joshua to thoroughly read and ponder the scriptures before entrusting him with the responsibility of leading the Israelites into the Promised Land. He was told by God to think about the book constantly. He did this to strengthen his spiritual endurance so that he could complete his task.

*"Like newborn babies, you must crave pure spiritual milk so that you will grow into a full experience of salvation. ""Cry out for his nourishment, now that you have had a taste of the Lord's kindness." 1 Peter 2:2–3 NLT.*

*"Like new born babies, you should crave thirst for, [earnestly desire] the pure [unadulterated] spiritual milk, that by it you may be nurtured and grow into [completed] salvation, since you have [already] tasted the goodness and kindness of the Lord". [Ps. 34:8] 1 Peter 2:2–3 AMPC*

Here, the Bible makes a demand of the faithful. It is essential to learn from and ingest God's words if you want to develop. This implies that no Christian can grow spiritually apart from feeding on the written word of God. By reading and examining God's word, Daniel was able to unravel the causes of the Jews' issues.

*"In the first year of his reign, I Daniel understood from the books the number of years that, according to the word of the Lord to Jeremiah the prophet, must pass by before the desolations [which had been] pronounced*

*on Jerusalem should end, and it was seventy years." [Jeremiah 25:11; 29:10]*
*Daniel 9:2 AMPC*

When Daniel was studying the Bible, he came across the prophecy regarding the Jews' seventy-year captivity in Babylon. Daniel was not yet born when this prophecy was written. But as he read the Bible, he became aware of it, which increased his faith and led him to ask God to pardon his people's sins.

Prayers:

*"And he spake a parable unto them to this end, that men ought always to pray and not to faint." Luke 18:1 KJV*

Jesus Christ commanded his followers to never stop praying. Many Christians are unaware of the significance of prayer. Nobody can be a successful true believer if they don't have a disciplined prayer life. Fainting indicates that forces are working to weaken or slack off people during prayer.

The devil does not want people to pray for many reasons. This is why he attacks people's prayer lives in many ways. Satan engages people in other things to divert their attention from praying to God. Prayer is one of the ways to build spiritual stamina. Prayer is the powerhouse of every Christian who inclines towards it. The Bible says:

*"Praying always with all prayer and supplication in the spirit, and watching thereunto with all perseverance and supplication for all the saints." Ephesians 6:18 KJV*

Prayer was a way of life for the Apostle Paul. One of the key elements of his success was prayer. The power of prayer was known to him. In order to fulfil their expectations, he counselled believers to always pray. Having served as a soldier for Jesus Christ, Paul was able to offer advice. Every situation we face in life requires prayer.

William Cowper wrote, "Satan trembles when he sees the weakest saint on his knees. Benny Hinn said, "When we pray, we disarm Satan and his agents." The Bible wants us to pray all types of prayers.

Here, I want to discuss seven different types of prayer. The opening prayer is a universal prayer for communion. Supplication is the act of raising your hands to God in prayer. A prayer of intercession followed. This entails supplication on other people's behalf. Dealing with Satan and demons is part of spiritual warfare. binding and expelling them, as well as releasing the oppressed. At least two people are required for a prayer of agreement to be effective. The final step is a prayer of thanks. It entails thanking God for all that He has done for us.

Fortify Yourself:

Engage yourself in things that strengthen your spirituality. Pray always, and worship God as you pray. To make your prayer more effective, pray using God's word. Endeavour to fellowship with other believers.

Make spiritual exercise a daily priority.

To aid in your growth, schedule specific times for prayer and Bible study and stick to the schedule. Try to read your Bible every day, and as you do, declare the Bible to be the inspired word of God. Do not be self-centred in your prayers. Pray for those in your neighbourhood, the world, and your nation.

Kindly close the book now and start praying as the Lord leads you.

# About The Author

Freeson U. Eze is not just a teacher of the word of God but a dedicated preacher of the gospel, driven by a profound passion to guide believers towards victorious living in Christ. His profound teachings are firmly rooted in the transformative power of God's word.

At the core of his ministry is a weekly programme where he shares insights and wisdom, alongside his authorship of the impactful book "The Spiritual Stamina for End-Time Christians." Freeson doesn't just stop at teaching; he actively engages in various ministries, notably serving as the director of KACY-I, a ministry committed to evangelism and missions.

Beyond his ministry endeavours, Freeson finds fulfilment in his family life, being happily married to Queen Eze, with whom he shares the joy of raising three sons. For those seeking guidance or wishing to connect, Freeson warmly invites you to reach out via email at spiritualstamina2021@gmail.com or efreeson@gmail.com.

# *Order Books By the Author*

Book Title: Marriage Medicine Vol 1

www.ingramcontent.com/pod-product-compliance
Lightning Source LLC
Chambersburg PA
CBHW060921140726
47996CB00001B/329